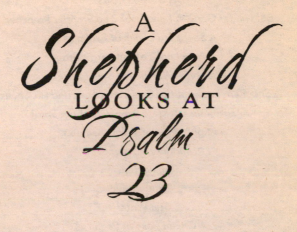

A
Shepherd
LOOKS AT
Psalm
23

By the Author ...

W. PHILLIP KELLER

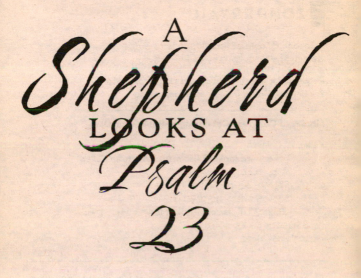

A Shepherd
LOOKS AT
Psalm
23

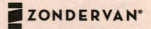

ZONDERVAN®

ZONDERVAN.com/
AUTHORTRACKER
follow your favorite authors

ZONDERVAN®

A Shepherd Looks at Psalm 23
Copyright © 1970, 2007 by W. Phillip Keller

Requests for information should be addressed to:
Zondervan, *Grand Rapids, Michigan* 49530

Library of Congress Cataloging-in-Publication Data

Keller, W. Phillip.
        A shepherd looks at Psalm 23 / W. Phillip Keller.
            p.   cm.
        ISBN-10: 0-310-27441-9
        ISBN-13: 978-0-310-27441-4
        1. Bible. O. T. Psalms XXIII — Meditations.   I. Title.
    BS145023rd.K43 2007
    223'.206 — dc22

                                                            2006102156

Interior design by Melissa Elenbaas

Printed in the United States of America

18 QGM 35

In tribute to "Chic"

who during many years of

adventure was my beloved

mate and companion

CONTENTS

INTRODUCTION

To a great extent the Bible is a collection of books written by men of humble origin, who penned under the guidance of God's Spirit. Much of its terminology and teaching is couched in rural language, dealing with outdoor subjects and natural phenomena. The audience to whom these writings were originally addressed were for the most part themselves simple, nomadic folk familiar with nature and the outdoor life of the countryside about them.

Today this is not the case. Many who either read or study the Scriptures in the twentieth century come from an urban, man-made environment. City people, especially, are often unfamiliar with such subjects as livestock, crops, land, fruit, or wildlife. They miss much of the truth taught in God's Word because they are not familiar with such things as sheep, wheat, soil, or grapes.

Yet divine revelation is irrevocably bound up with the basic subjects of the natural world. Our Lord Himself, when He was amongst us, continually used natural phenomena to explain supernatural truth in His parables. It is a sound, indisputable method, both scientifically and spiritually valid.

All this is understandable and meaningful when we recognize the fact that God is author and originator of both the natural and supernatural (spiritual). The same basic laws, principles, and procedures function in these two contiguous realms.

Therefore it follows that to understand one is to grasp the parallel principle in the other.

It must be stated here that it is through this type of scriptural interpretation that my own understanding of the Bible has become meaningful. It explains in part, too, why truths which I shared with various audiences have been long remembered by them with great clarity.

Accordingly I make no apologies for presenting this collection of "shepherd insights" into the well-known and loved—but often misunderstood—23rd Psalm.

This book has been developed against a rather unique background which has perhaps given me a deeper appreciation than most men of what David had in mind when he wrote his beautiful poem. First of all, I grew up and lived in East Africa, surrounded by simple native herders whose customs closely resembled those of their counterparts in the Middle East. So I am intimately acquainted with the romance, the pathos, the picturesque life of an Eastern shepherd. Secondly, as a young man, I actually made my own livelihood for about eight years as a sheep owner and sheep rancher. Consequently I write as one who has had firsthand experience with every phase of sheep management. Later, as the lay pastor of a community church, I shared the truths of this Psalm, as a shepherd, with my "flock," every Sunday for several months.

It is, therefore, out of the variety of these firsthand experiences with sheep that the following chapters have emerged. To my knowledge this is the first time that a down-to-earth, hard-handed sheepman has ever written at length about the Shepherd's Psalm.

There is one difficulty that arises when writing a book based on a familiar portion of the Scriptures. One disillusions or disenchants the reader with some of his former notions about the Psalm. Like much spiritual teaching, the 23rd Psalm has had a certain amount of sentimental imagery wrapped around it with no sound basis in actual life. Some ideas advanced about it have, in fact, been almost ludicrous.

I would ask, then, that the reader approach the pages that follow with an open mind and an unbiased spirit. If he does, fresh truth and exciting glimpses of God's care and concern for him will flood over his being. Then he will be brought into a bold, new appreciation of the endless effort put forth by our Saviour for His sheep. Out of this there will then emerge a growing admiration and affection for the Great Shepherd of his soul.

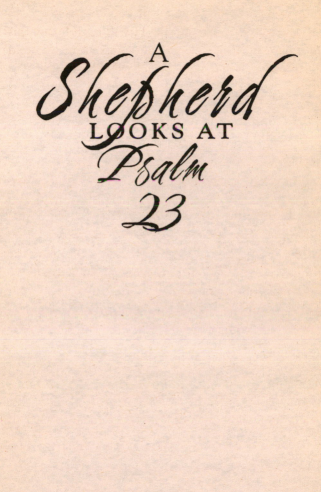

A Shepherd LOOKS AT Psalm 23

"THE LORD IS MY SHEPHERD"

The Lord! But who is the Lord? What is His character? Does He have adequate credentials to be my Shepherd—my manager—my owner?

And if He does—how do I come under His control? In what way do I become the object of His concern and diligent care?

These are penetrating, searching questions, and they deserve honest and basic examination.

One of the calamities of Christianity is our tendency to talk in ambiguous generalities.

David, the author of the poem, himself a shepherd and the son of a shepherd, later to be known as the "Shepherd King" of Israel, stated explicitly, "The Lord is my shepherd." To whom did he refer?

He referred to Jehovah, the Lord God of Israel.

His statement was confirmed by Jesus the Christ. When He was God incarnate amongst men, He declared emphatically, "I am the good shepherd."

But who was this Christ?

Our view of Him is often too small—too cramped—too provincial—too human.

And because it is, we feel unwilling to allow Him to have authority or control—much less outright ownership of our lives.

He it was who was directly responsible for the creation of all things both natural and supernatural (see Colossians 1:15–20).

If we pause to reflect on the person of Christ—on His power and His achievements—suddenly like David we will be glad to state proudly, "The Lord—*He* is my Shepherd!"

But before we do this it helps to hold clearly in mind the particular part played upon our history by God the Father, God the Son, and God the Holy Spirit.

God the Father is God the author—the originator of all that exists. It was in His mind, first, that all took shape.

God the Son, our Saviour, is God the artisan—the artist, the Creator of all that exists. He brought into being all that had been originally formulated in His Father's mind.

God the Holy Spirit is God the agent who presents these facts to both my mind and my spiritual understanding so that they become both real and relative to me as an individual.

Now the beautiful relationships given to us repeatedly in Scripture between God and man are those of a father to his children and a shepherd to his sheep. These concepts were first conceived in the mind of God our Father. They were made possible and practical through the work of Christ. They are confirmed and made real in me through the agency of the gracious Holy Spirit.

So when the simple—though sublime—statement is made by a man or woman that "The Lord is my shepherd," it immediately implies a profound yet practical working relationship between a human being and his Maker.

It links a lump of common clay to divine destiny—it means a mere mortal becomes the cherished object of divine diligence.

This thought alone should stir my spirit, quicken my own sense of awareness, and lend enormous dignity to myself as an individual. To think that God in Christ is deeply concerned about me as a particular person immediately gives great purpose and enormous meaning to my short sojourn upon this planet.

And the greater, the wider, the more majestic my concept is of the Christ—the more vital will be my relationship to Him. Obviously, David, in this Psalm, is speaking not as the shepherd, though he was one, but as a sheep, one of the flock. He spoke with a strong sense of pride and devotion and admiration. It was as though he literally boasted aloud, "Look at who my shepherd is—my owner— my manager!" The Lord is!

After all, he knew from firsthand experience that the lot in life of any particular sheep depended on the type of man who owned it. Some men were gentle, kind, intelligent, brave, and selfless in their devotion to their stock. Under one man sheep would struggle, starve, and suffer endless hardship. In another's care they would flourish and thrive contentedly.

So if the Lord is my Shepherd I should know something of His character and understand something of His ability.

To meditate on this I frequently go out at night to walk alone under the stars and remind myself of His majesty and might. Looking up at the star-studded sky I remember that at least 250,000,000 x 250,000,000 such bodies—each larger than our sun, one of the smallest of the stars—have been scattered across the vast spaces of the universe by His hand. I recall that the planet earth, which is my temporary home for a few short years, is so minute a speck of matter in space that if it were possible to transport our most powerful telescope to our nearest neighbor star, Alpha Centauri, and look back this way, the earth could not be seen, even with the aid of that powerful instrument.

All this is a bit humbling. It drains the "ego" from a man and puts things in proper perspective. It makes me see myself as a mere mite of material in an enormous universe. Yet the staggering fact remains that Christ, the Creator of such an enormous universe of overwhelming magnitude, deigns to call Himself my Shepherd and invites me to consider myself His sheep—His special object of affection and attention. Who better could care for me?

By the same sort of process I stoop down and pick up a handful of soil from the backyard or roadside. Placing it under an electron microscope I am astounded to discover it teems with billions upon billions of micro-organisms. Many of them are so complex in their own peculiar cellular structure that even a fraction of their functions in the earth are not yet properly understood.

Yes, He the Christ—the Son of God—brought all of this into being. From the most gigantic galaxy to the most minute microbe, all function flawlessly in accordance with definite laws of order and unity which are utterly beyond the mind of finite man to master.

It is in this sense, first of all, that I am basically bound to admit that His ownership of me as a human being is legitimate—simply because it is He who brought me into being and no one is better able to understand or care for me.

I belong to Him simply because He deliberately chose to create me as the object of His own affection.

It is patently clear that most men and women refuse to acknowledge this fact. Their deliberate attempts to deny that such a relationship even exists or could exist between a man and his Maker demonstrate their abhorrence of admitting that anyone really can claim ownership or authority over them by virtue of bringing them into being.

This was of course the enormous "risk" or "calculated chance," if we may use the term, which God took in making man initially.

But in His usual magnanimous manner He took the second step in attempting to restore this relationship which is repeatedly breached by men who turn their backs on Him.

Again in Christ He demonstrated at Calvary the deep desire of His heart to have men come under His benevolent care. He Himself absorbed the penalty for their perverseness, stating clearly that "we all, like sheep, have gone astray, each of us has turned to his own way; and the Lord has laid on him the iniquity of us all" (Isaiah 53:6).

Thus, in a second very real and vital sense I truly belong to Him simply because He has bought me again at the incredible price of His own laid-down life and shed blood.

Therefore He was entitled to say, "I am the good shepherd. The good shepherd lays down his life for the sheep."

So there remains the moving realization that we have been bought with a price, that we are really not our own and He is well within His rights to lay claim upon our lives.

I recall quite clearly how in my first venture with sheep, the question of paying a price for my ewes was so terribly important. They belonged to me only by virtue of the fact that I paid hard cash for them. It was money earned by the blood and sweat and tears drawn from my own body during the desperate grinding years of the Depression. And when I bought that first small flock I was buying them literally with my own body which had been laid down with this day in mind.

Because of this I felt in a special way that they were in very truth a part of me and I a part of them. There was an intimate identity involved which, though not apparent on the surface to the casual observer, nonetheless made those thirty ewes exceedingly precious to me.

But the day I bought them I also realized that this was but the first stage in a long, lasting endeavor in which from then on, I would, as their owner, have to continually lay down my life for them if they were to flourish and prosper. Sheep do not "just take care of themselves" as some might suppose. They require, more than any other class of livestock, endless attention and meticulous care.

It is no accident that God has chosen to call us sheep. The behavior of sheep and human beings is similar in many ways as will be seen in further chapters. Our mass mind (or mob instincts), our fears and timidity, our stubbornness and stupidity, our perverse habits are all parallels of profound importance.

Yet despite these adverse characteristics Christ chooses us, buys us, calls us by name, makes us His own, and delights in caring for us.

It is this last aspect which is really the third reason why we are under obligation to recognize His ownership of us. He literally lays Himself out for us continually. He is ever interceding for us; He is ever guiding us by His gracious Spirit; He is ever working on our behalf to ensure that we will benefit from His care.

In fact, Psalm 23 might well be called "David's Hymn of Praise to Divine Diligence." For the entire poem goes on to recount the manner in which the Good Shepherd spares no pains for the welfare of His sheep.

Little wonder that the poet took pride in belonging to the Good Shepherd. Why shouldn't he?

In memory I can still see one of the sheep ranches in our district which was operated by a tenant sheepman. He ought never to have been allowed to keep sheep. His stock were always thin, weak, and riddled with disease or parasites. Again and again they would come and stand at the fence staring blankly through the woven wire at the green lush pastures which my flock enjoyed. Had they been able to speak I am sure they would have said, "Oh, to be set free from this awful owner!"

This is a picture which has never left my memory. It is a picture of pathetic people the world over who have not known what it is to belong to the Good Shepherd ... who suffer instead under sin and Satan.

How amazing it is that individual men and women vehemently refuse and reject the claims of Christ on their lives. They fear that to acknowledge His ownership is to come under the rule of a tyrant.

This is difficult to comprehend when one pauses to consider the character of Christ. Admittedly there have been many false caricatures of this Person, but an unbiased look at His life quickly reveals an individual of enormous compassion and incredible integrity.

He was the most balanced and perhaps the most beloved being ever to enter the society of men. Though born amid most disgusting surroundings, the member of a modest working family, He bore Himself always with great dignity and assurance. Though He enjoyed no special advantages as a child, either in education or employment, His entire philosophy and outlook on life were the highest standards of human conduct ever set before mankind. Though He had no vast economic assets, political power, or military might, no other person ever made such an enormous impact on the world's history. Because of Him, millions of people across almost twenty centuries of time have come into a life of decency and honor and noble conduct.

Not only was He gentle and tender and true but also righteous, stern as steel, and terribly tough on phony people.

He was magnificent in His magnanimous spirit of forgiveness for fallen folk but a terror to those who indulged in double talk or false pretenses.

He came to set men free from their own sins, their own selves, their own fears. Those so liberated loved Him with fierce loyalty.

It is this One who insists that He was the Good Shepherd, the understanding Shepherd, the concerned Shepherd who cares enough to seek out and save and restore lost men and women.

He never hesitated to make it quite clear that when an individual once came under His management and control there would be a certain new and unique relationship between Him and them. There would be something very special about belonging to this particular Shepherd. There would be a distinct mark upon the man or woman that differentiated him or her from the rest of the crowd.

The day I bought my first thirty ewes, my neighbor and I sat on the dusty corral rails that enclosed the sheep pens and admired the choice, strong, well-bred ewes that had become mine. Turning to me he handed me a large, sharp, killing knife and remarked tersely, "Well, Phillip, they're yours. Now you'll have to put your mark on them."

I knew exactly what he meant. Each shepherd has his own distinctive earmark which he cuts into one of the ears of his sheep. In this way, even at a distance, it is easy to determine to whom the sheep belongs.

It was not the most pleasant procedure to catch each ewe in turn and lay her ear on a wooden block, then notch it deeply with the razor-sharp edge of the knife. There was pain for both of us. But from our mutual suffering an indelible lifelong mark of ownership was made that could never be erased. And from then on every sheep that came into my possession would bear my mark.

There is an exciting parallel to this in the Old Testament. When a slave in any Hebrew household chose, of his own free will, to become a lifetime member of that home, he was subjected to a certain ritual. His master and owner would take him to his door, put his ear lobe against the door post and with an awl puncture a hole through the ear. From then on he was a man marked for life as belonging to that house.

For the man or woman who recognizes the claim of Christ and gives allegiance to His absolute ownership, there comes the question of bearing His mark. The mark of the cross is that which should identify us with Him for all time. The question is—does it?

Jesus made it clear when He stated emphatically, "If anyone would come after me, he must deny himself and take up his cross daily and follow me."

Basically what it amounts to is this: A person exchanges the fickle fortunes of living life by sheer whimsy for the more productive and satisfying adventure of being guided by God.

It is a tragic truth that many people who really have never come under His direction or management claim that "The Lord is my shepherd." They seem to hope that by merely admitting that He is their Shepherd somehow they will enjoy the benefits of His care and management without paying the price of forfeiting their own fickle and foolish way of life.

One cannot have it both ways. Either we belong or we don't. Jesus Himself warned us that there would come a day when many would say, "Lord, in Your name we did many wonderful things," but He will retort that He never knew us as His own.

It is a most serious and sobering thought which should make us search our own hearts and motives and personal relationship to Him.

Do I really belong to Him?

Do I really recognize His right to me?

Do I respond to His authority and acknowledge His ownership?

Do I find freedom and complete fulfillment in this arrangement?

Do I sense a purpose and deep contentment because I am under His direction?

Do I know rest and repose, besides a definite sense of exciting adventure, in belonging to Him?

If so, then with genuine gratitude and exaltation I can exclaim proudly, just as David did, "The Lord is my shepherd!" and I'm thrilled to belong to Him, for it is thus that I shall flourish and thrive no matter what life may bring to me.

"I SHALL NOT BE
IN WANT"

*W*hat a proud, positive, bold statement to make! Obviously, this is the sentiment of a sheep utterly satisfied with its owner, perfectly content with its lot in life.

Since the Lord is my Shepherd, then I shall not want. Actually the word "want," as used here, has a broader meaning than might at first be imagined. No doubt the main concept is that of not lacking— not deficient—in proper care, management, or husbandry.

But a second emphasis is the idea of being utterly contented in the Good Shepherd's care and consequently not craving or desiring anything more.

This may seem a strange statement for a man like David to have made if we think in terms only of physical or material needs. After all, he had been hounded and harried repeatedly by the forces of his enemy Saul as well as by those of his own estranged son Absalom. He was obviously a man who had known intense privation: deep personal poverty, acute hardship, and anguish of spirit.

Therefore it is absurd to assert on the basis of this statement that the child of God, the sheep in the Shepherd's care, will never experience lack or need.

It is imperative to keep a balanced view of the Christian life. To do this it is well to consider the careers of men like Elijah, John the Baptist, our Lord Himself—and even modern men of faith such as Livingstone—to realize that all of them experienced great personal privation and adversity.

When He was among us, the Great Shepherd Himself warned His disciples before His departure for glory, that—"In this world you will have trouble. But take heart! I have overcome the world."

One of the fallacies that is common among Christians today is the assertion that if a man or woman is prospering materially it is a significant mark of the blessing of God upon his or her life. This simply is not so.

Rather, in bold contrast we read in Revelation 3:17, "You say, 'I am rich; I have acquired wealth and do not need a thing.' But you do not realize that you are wretched, pitiful, poor, blind and naked."

Or, in an equally pointed way, Jesus made clear to the rich young ruler who wished to become His follower, "One thing you lack.... Go, sell everything you have and give to the poor.... Then come, follow me" (Mark 10:21).

Based on the teachings of the Bible we can only conclude that David was not referring to material or physical poverty when he made the statement, "I shall not be in want."

For this very reason the Christian has to take a long, hard look at life. He has to recognize that as with many of God's choice people before him, he may be called on to experience lack of wealth or material benefits. He has to see his sojourn upon the planet as a brief interlude during which there may well be some privation in a physical sense. Yet amid such hardship he can still boast, "*I shall not want ... I shall not lack* the expert care and management of my Master."

To grasp the inner significance of this simple statement it is necessary to understand the difference between belonging to one master or another — to the Good Shepherd or to an imposter. Jesus Himself took great pains to point out to anyone who contemplated following Him that it was quite impossible to serve two masters. One belonged either to Him or to another.

When all is said and done, the welfare of any flock is entirely dependent upon the management afforded them by their owner.

The tenant sheepman on the farm next to my first ranch was the most indifferent manager I had ever met. He was not concerned about the condition of his sheep. His land was neglected. He gave little or no time to his flock, letting them pretty well forage for themselves as best they could, both summer and winter. They fell prey to dogs, cougars, and rustlers.

Every year these poor creatures were forced to gnaw away at bare brown fields and impoverished pastures. Every winter there was a shortage of nourishing hay and wholesome grain to feed the hungry ewes. Shelter to safeguard and protect the suffering sheep from storms and blizzards was scanty and inadequate.

They had only polluted, muddy water to drink. There had been a lack of salt and other trace minerals needed to offset their sickly pastures. In their thin, weak, and diseased condition these poor sheep were a pathetic sight.

In my mind's eye I can still see them standing at the fence, huddled sadly in little knots, staring wistfully through the wires at the rich pastures on the other side.

To all their distress, the heartless, selfish owner seemed utterly callous and indifferent. He simply did not care. What if his sheep did *want* green grass, fresh water, shade, safety, or shelter from the storms? What if they did *want* relief from wounds, bruises, disease, and parasites?

He ignored their needs—he couldn't care less. Why should he—they were just sheep—fit only for the slaughterhouse.

I never looked at those poor sheep without an acute awareness that this was a precise picture of those wretched old taskmasters, Sin and Satan, on their derelict ranch—scoffing at the plight of those within their power.

As I have moved among men and women from all strata of society as both a lay pastor and as a scientist, I have become increasingly aware of one thing. It is the boss—the manager—the Master in people's lives who makes the difference in their destiny.

I have known some of the wealthiest men on this continent intimately—also some of the leading scientists and professional people. Despite their dazzling outward show of success, despite their affluence and their prestige, they remained poor in spirit, shriveled in soul, and unhappy in life. They were joyless people held in the iron grip and heartless ownership of the wrong master.

By way of contrast, I have numerous friends among relatively poor people—people who have known hardship, disaster, and the struggle to stay afloat financially. But because they belong to Christ and have recognized Him as Lord and Master of their lives, their owner and manager, they are permeated by a deep, quiet, settled peace that is beautiful to behold.

It is indeed a delight to visit some of these humble homes where men and women are rich in spirit, generous in heart, and large of soul. They radiate a serene confidence and quiet joy that surmounts all the tragedies of their time.

They are under God's care and they know it. They have entrusted themselves to Christ's control and found contentment.

Contentment should be the hallmark of the man or woman who has put his or her affairs in the hands of God. This especially applies in our affluent age. But the outstanding paradox is the intense fever of discontent among people who are ever speaking of security.

Despite an unparalleled wealth in material assets, we are outstandingly insecure and unsure of ourselves and well nigh bankrupt in spiritual values.

Always men are searching for safety beyond themselves. They are restless, unsettled, covetous, greedy for more—wanting this and that, yet never really satisfied in spirit.

By contrast the simple Christian, the humble person, the Shepherd's sheep, can stand up proudly and boast.

"The Lord is my shepherd—I shall not be in want."

I am completely satisfied with His management of my life. Why? Because He is the sheepman to whom no trouble is too great as He cares for His flock. He is the rancher who is outstanding because of His fondness for sheep—Who loves them for their own sake as well as His personal pleasure in them. He will, if necessary, be on the job twenty-four hours a day to see that they are properly provided for in every detail. Above all, He is very jealous of His name and high reputation as "The Good Shepherd."

He is the owner who delights in His flock. For Him there is no greater reward, no deeper satisfaction, than that of seeing His sheep contented, well fed, safe, and flourishing under His care. This is indeed His very "life." He gives all He has to it. He literally lays Himself out for those who are His.

He will go to no end of trouble and labor to supply them with the finest grazing, the richest pasturage, ample winter feed, and clean water. He will spare Himself no pains to provide shelter from storms, protection from ruthless enemies and the diseases and parasites to which sheep are so susceptible.

No wonder Jesus said, "I am the good shepherd. The good shepherd lays down his life for the sheep."

And again, "I have come that they may have life, and have it to the full."

From early dawn until late at night this utterly selfless Shepherd is alert to the welfare of His flock. For the diligent sheepman rises early and goes out first thing every morning without fail to look over his flock. It is the initial, intimate contact of the day. With a practiced, searching, sympathetic eye he examines the sheep to see that they are fit and content and able to be on their feet. In an instant he can tell if they have been molested during the night—whether any are ill or if there are some which require special attention.

Repeatedly throughout the day he casts his eye over the flock to make sure that all is well.

Nor even at night is he oblivious to their needs. He sleeps as it were "with one eye and both ears open," ready at the least sign of trouble to leap up and protect his own.

This is a sublime picture of the care given to those whose lives are under Christ's control. He knows all about their lives from morning to night.

"Praise be to the Lord, to God our Savior, who daily bears our burdens."

"He who watches over you will not slumber."

In spite of having such a master and owner, the fact remains that some Christians are still not content with His control. They are somewhat dissatisfied, always feeling that somehow the grass beyond the fence must be a little greener. These are carnal Christians—one might almost call them "fence crawlers" or "half-Christians" who want the best of both worlds.

I once owned a ewe whose conduct exactly typified this sort of person. She was one of the most attractive sheep that ever belonged to me. Her body was beautifully proportioned. She had a strong constitution and an excellent coat of wool. Her head was clean, alert, well-set with bright eyes. She bore sturdy lambs that matured rapidly.

But in spite of all these attractive attributes she had one pronounced fault.

She was restless—discontent—a fence crawler.

So much so that I came to call her "Mrs. Gad-about."

This one ewe produced more problems for me than almost all the rest of the flock combined.

No matter what field or pasture the sheep were in, she would search all along the fences or shoreline (we lived by the sea) looking for a loophole she could crawl through and start to feed on the other side.

It was not that she lacked pasturage. My fields were my joy and delight. No sheep in the district had better grazing.

With "Mrs. Gad-about" it was an ingrained habit. She was simply never contented with things as they were. Often when she had forced her way through some such spot in a fence or found a way around the end of the wire at low tide on the beaches, she would end up feeding on bare, brown, burned-up pasturage of a most inferior sort.

But she never learned her lesson and continued to fence crawl time after time.

Now it would have been bad enough if she was the only one who did this. It was a sufficient problem to find her and bring her back. But the further point was that she taught her lambs the same tricks. They simply followed her example and soon were as skilled at escaping as their mother.

Even worse, however, was the example she set for the other sheep. In short time she began to lead others through the same holes and over the same dangerous paths down by the sea.

After putting up with her perverseness for a summer, I finally came to the conclusion that to save the rest of the flock from becoming unsettled, she would have to go. I could not allow one obstinate, discontented ewe to ruin the whole ranch operation.

It was a difficult decision to make, for I loved her in the same way I loved the rest. Her strength and beauty and alertness were a delight to the eye.

But one morning I took the killing knife in hand and butchered her. Her career of fence crawling was cut short. It was the only solution to the dilemma.

She was a sheep, who, in spite of all that I had done to give her the very best care, still wanted something else.

She was not like the one who said, "The Lord is my shepherd—I shall not be in want."

It is a solemn warning to the carnal Christian—backslider—the half-Christian—the one who wants the best of both worlds.

Sometimes in short order they can be cut down.

"HE MAKES ME LIE DOWN IN GREEN PASTURES"

The strange thing about sheep is that because of their very makeup it is almost impossible for them to be made to lie down unless four requirements are met.

Owing to their timidity they refuse to lie down unless they are free of all fear.

Because of the social behavior within a flock, sheep will not lie down unless they are free from friction with others of their kind.

If tormented by flies or parasites, sheep will not lie down. Only when free of these pests can they relax.

Lastly, sheep will not lie down as long as they feel in need of finding food. They must be free from hunger.

It is significant that to be at rest there must be a definite sense of freedom from fear, tension, aggravations, and hunger. The unique aspect of the picture is that it is only the sheepman himself who can provide release from these anxieties. It all depends upon the diligence of the owner whether or not his flock is free of disturbing influences.

When we examine each of these four factors that affect sheep so severely we will understand why the part the owner plays in their management is so tremendously important. It is actually he who makes it possible for them to lie down, to rest, to relax, to be content and quiet and flourishing.

A flock that is restless, discontented, always agitated and disturbed never does well.

And the same is true of people.

It is not generally known that sheep are so timid and easily panicked that even a stray jackrabbit suddenly bounding from behind a bush can stampede a whole flock. When one startled sheep runs in fright a dozen others will bolt with it in blind fear, not waiting to see what frightened them.

One day a friend came to call on us from the city. She had a tiny Pekingese pup along. As she opened the car door the pup jumped out on the grass. Just one glimpse of the unexpected little dog was enough. In terror over two hundred of my sheep which were resting nearby leaped up and rushed off across the pasture.

As long as there is even the slightest suspicion of danger from dogs, coyotes, cougars, bears, or other enemies the sheep stand up ready to flee for their lives. They have little or no means of self-defense. They are helpless, timid, feeble creatures whose only recourse is to run.

When I invited friends to visit us, after the Pekingese episode, I always made it clear their dogs were to be left at home. I also had to drive off or shoot other stray dogs that came to molest or disturb the sheep. Two dogs have been known to kill as many as 292 sheep in a single night of unbridled slaughter.

Ewes, heavy in lamb, when chased by dogs or other predators, will slip their unborn lambs and lose them in abortions. A shepherd's loss from such forays can be appalling. One morning at dawn I found nine of my choicest ewes, all soon to lamb, lying dead in the field where a cougar had harried the flock during the night.

It was a terrible shock to a young man like myself just new to the business and unfamiliar with such attacks. From then on I slept with a .303 rifle and flashlight by my bed. At the least sound of the flock being disturbed I would leap from bed and, calling my faithful collie, dash out into the night, rifle in hand, ready to protect my sheep.

In the course of time I came to realize that nothing so quieted and reassured the sheep as to see me in the field. The presence of their master and owner and protector put them at ease as nothing else could do, and this applied day and night.

There was one summer when sheep rustling was a common occurrence in our district. Night after night the dog and I were out under the stars, keeping watch over the flock by night, ready to defend them from the raids of any rustlers. The news of my diligence spread along the grapevine of our back country roads, and the rustlers quickly decided to leave us alone and try their tactics elsewhere.

"He makes me lie down."

In the Christian's life there is no substitute for the keen awareness that my Shepherd is nearby. There is nothing like Christ's presence to dispel the fear, the panic, the terror of the unknown.

We live a most uncertain life. Any hour can bring disaster, danger, and distress from unknown quarters. Life is full of hazards. No one can tell what a day will produce in new trouble. We live either in a sense of anxiety, fear, and foreboding, or in a sense of quiet rest. Which is it?

Generally it is the "unknown," the "unexpected," that produces the greatest panic. It is in the grip of fear that most of us are unable to cope with the cruel circumstances and harsh complexities of life. We feel they are foes which endanger our tranquillity.

Often our first impulse is simply to get up and run from them.

Then in the midst of our misfortunes there suddenly comes the awareness that He, the Christ, the Good Shepherd, is there. It makes all the difference. His presence in the picture throws a different light on the whole scene. Suddenly things are not half so black nor nearly so terrifying. The outlook changes and there is hope. I find myself delivered from fear. Rest returns and I can relax.

This has come to me again and again as I grow older. It is the knowledge that my Master, my Friend, my Owner has things under control even when they may appear calamitous. This gives me great consolation, repose, and rest. "Now I lay me down in peace and sleep, for Thou, God, keepest me."

It is the special office work of God's gracious Spirit to convey this sense of the Christ to our fearful hearts. He comes quietly to reassure us that Christ Himself is aware of our dilemma and deeply involved in it with us.

And it is in fact in this assurance that we rest and relax.

"For God did not give us a spirit of timidity, but a spirit of power, of love and of self-discipline" (2 Timothy 1:7).

The idea of a sound mind is that of a mind at ease—at peace—not perturbed or harassed or obsessed with fear and foreboding for the future.

"I will lie down and sleep in peace, for you alone, O Lord, make me dwell in safety."

The second source of fear from which the sheepman delivers his sheep is that of tension, rivalry, and cruel competition within the flock itself.

In every animal society there is established an order of dominance or status within the group. In a penful of chickens it is referred to as the "pecking order." With cattle it is called the "horning order." Among sheep we speak of the "butting order."

Generally an arrogant, cunning, and domineering old ewe will be boss of any bunch of sheep. She maintains her position of prestige by butting and driving other ewes or lambs away from the best grazing or favorite bedgrounds. Succeeding her in precise order the other sheep all establish and maintain their exact position in the flock by using the same tactics of butting and thrusting at those below and around them.

A vivid and accurate word picture of this process is given to us in Ezekiel 34:15–16 and 20–22. This is a startling example, in fact, of the scientific accuracy of the Scriptures in describing a natural phenomenon.

Because of this rivalry, tension, and competition for status and self-assertion, there is friction in the flock. The sheep cannot lie down and rest in contentment. Always they must stand up and defend their rights and contest the challenge of the intruder.

Hundreds and hundreds of times I have watched an austere old ewe walk up to a younger one which might have been feeding contentedly or resting quietly in some sheltered spot. She would arch her neck, tilt her head, dilate her eyes, and approach the other with a stiff-legged gait. All of this was saying in unmistakable terms, "Move over! Out of my way! Give ground or else!" And if the other ewe did not immediately leap to her feet in self-defense, she would be butted unmercifully. Or if she did rise to accept the challenge, one or two strong thrusts would soon send her scurrying for safety.

This continuous conflict and jealousy within the flock can be a most detrimental thing. The sheep become edgy, tense, discontented, and restless. They lose weight and become irritable.

But one point that always interested me very much was that whenever I came into view and my presence attracted their attention, the sheep quickly forgot their foolish rivalries and stopped their fighting. The shepherd's presence made all the difference in their behavior.

This, to me, has always been a graphic picture of the struggle for status in human society. There is the eternal competition "to keep up with the Joneses" or, as it is now—"to keep up with the Joneses' kids."

In any business firm, any office, any family, any community, any church, any human organization or group, be it large or small, the struggle for self-assertion and self-recognition goes on. Most of us fight to be "top sheep." We butt and quarrel and compete to "get ahead." And in the process people are hurt.

It is here that much jealousy arises. This is where petty peeves grow into horrible hate. It is where ill-will and contempt come into being, the place where heated rivalry and deep discontent is born. It is here that discontent gradually grows into a covetous way of life where one has to be forever "standing up" for himself, for his rights, "standing up" just to get ahead of the crowd.

In contrast to this, the picture in the Psalm shows us God's people lying down in quiet contentment.

One of the outstanding marks of a Christian should be a serene sense of gentle contentment.

"Godliness with contentment is great gain."

Paul put it this way, "I have learned to be content whatever the circumstances," and certainly this applies to my status in society.

The endless unrest generated in the individual who is always trying to "get ahead" of the crowd, who is attempting always to be top man or woman on the totem pole, is pretty formidable to observe.

In His own unique way, Jesus Christ, the Great Shepherd, in His earthly life pointed out that the last would be first and the first last. In a sense I am sure He meant first in the area of His own intimate affection. For any shepherd has great compassion for the poor, weak sheep that get butted about by the more domineering ones.

More than once I have strongly trounced a belligerent ewe for abusing a weaker one. Or when they butted lambs not their own I found it necessary to discipline them severely, and certainly they were not first in my esteem for their aggressiveness.

Another point that impressed me, too, was that the less aggressive sheep were often far more contented, quiet, and restful. So there were definite advantages in being "bottom sheep."

But more important was the fact that it was the shepherd's presence that put an end to all rivalry. And in our human relationships when we become acutely aware of being in the presence of Christ, our foolish, selfish snobbery and rivalry will end. It is the humble heart walking quietly and contentedly in the close and intimate companionship of Christ that is at rest, that can relax, simply glad to lie down and let the world go by.

When my eyes are on my Master they are not on those around me. This is the place of peace.

And it is good and proper to remind ourselves that in the end it is He who will decide and judge what my status really is. After all, it is His estimation of me that is of consequence. Any human measurement at best is bound to be pretty unpredictable, unreliable, and far from final.

To be thus, close to Him, conscious of His abiding Presence, made real in my mind, emotions, and will by the indwelling gracious Spirit, is to be set free from fear of my fellow man and whatever he might think of me.

I would much rather have the affection of the Good Shepherd than occupy a place of prominence in society ... especially if I had attained it by fighting, quarreling, and bitter rivalry with my fellow human beings.

"Blessed [happy, to be envied] are the merciful, for they will be shown mercy" (Matthew 5:7).

As is the case with freedom from fear of predators or friction within the flock, the freedom of fear from the torment of parasites and insects is essential to the contentment of sheep. This aspect of their behavior will be dealt with in greater detail later in the Psalm. But it is nevertheless important to mention it here.

Sheep, especially in the summer, can be driven to absolute distraction by nasal flies, bot flies, warble flies, and ticks. When tormented by these pests it is literally impossible for them to lie down and rest. Instead they are up and on their feet, stamping their legs, shaking their heads, ready to rush off into the bush for relief from the pests.

Only the diligent care of the owner who keeps a constant lookout for these insects will prevent them from annoying his flock. A good shepherd will apply various types of insect repellents to his sheep. He will see that they are dipped to clear their fleeces of ticks. And he will see that there are shelter belts of trees and bush available where they can find refuge and release from their tormentors.

This all entails considerable extra care. It takes time and labor and expensive chemicals to do the job thoroughly. It means, too, that the sheepman must be amongst his charges daily, keeping a close watch on their behavior. As soon as there is the least evidence that they are being disturbed he must take steps to provide them with relief. Always uppermost in his mind is the aim of keeping his flock quiet, contented, and at peace.

Similarly in the Christian life there are bound to be many small irritations. There are the annoyances of petty frustrations and ever-recurring disagreeable experiences.

In modern terminology we refer to these upsetting circumstances or people as "being bugged."

Is there an antidote for them?

Can one come to the place of quiet contentment despite them?

The answer, for the one in Christ's care, is definitely "Yes!"

This is one of the main functions of the gracious Holy Spirit. In Scripture He is often symbolized by oil — by that which brings healing and comfort and relief from the harsh and abrasive aspects of life.

The gracious Holy Spirit makes real in me the very presence of the Christ. He brings quietness, serenity, strength, and calmness in the face of frustrations and futility.

When I turn to Him and expose the problem to Him, allowing Him to see that I have a dilemma, a difficulty, a disagreeable experience beyond my control, He comes to assist. Often a helpful approach is simply to say aloud, "O Master, this is beyond me—I can't cope with it—it's bugging me—I can't rest—please take over!"

Then He does take over in His own wondrous way. He applies the healing, soothing, effective antidote of His own person and presence to my particular problem. There immediately comes into my consciousness the awareness of His dealing with the difficulty in a way I had not anticipated. And because of the assurance that He has become active on my behalf, there steals over me a sense of quiet contentment. I am then able to lie down in peace and rest. All because of what He does.

Finally, to produce the conditions necessary for a sheep to lie down there must be freedom from the fear of hunger. This of course is clearly implied in the statement, "He makes me lie down in green pastures."

It is not generally recognized that many of the great sheep countries of the world are dry, semi-arid areas. Most breeds of sheep flourish best in this sort of terrain. They are susceptible to fewer hazards of health or parasites where the climate is dry. But in those same regions it is neither natural nor common to find green pastures. For example, Palestine, where David wrote this Psalm and kept his father's flocks, especially near Bethlehem, is a dry, brown, sun-burned wasteland.

Green pastures did not just happen by chance. Green pastures were the product of tremendous labor, time, and skill in land use. Green pastures were the result of clearing rough, rocky land; of tearing out brush and roots and stumps; of deep plowing and careful soil preparation; of seeding and planting special grains and legumes; of irrigating with water and husbanding with care the crops of forage that would feed the flocks.

All of this represented tremendous toil and skill and time for the careful shepherd. If his sheep were to enjoy green pastures amid the brown, barren hills, it meant he had a tremendous job to do.

But green pastures are essential to success with sheep. When lambs are maturing and the ewes need green, succulent feed for a heavy milk flow, there is no substitute for good pasturage. No sight so satisfies the sheep owner as to see his flock well and quietly fed to repletion on rich green forage, able to lie down to rest, ruminate, and gain.

In my own ranching operations, one of the keys to the entire enterprise lay in developing rich, lush pastures for my flock. On at least two ranches there were old, worn out, impoverished fields that were either bare or infested with inferior forage plants. By skillful management and scientific land use these were soon converted into flourishing fields knee deep in rich green grass and legumes. On such forage it was common to have lambs reach 100 pounds in weight within 100 days from birth.

The secret to this was that the flock could fill up quickly, then lie down quietly to rest and ruminate.

A hungry, ill-fed sheep is ever on its feet, on the move, searching for another scanty mouthful of forage to try and satisfy its gnawing hunger. Such sheep are not contented, they do not thrive, they are of no use to themselves nor to their owners. They languish and lack vigor and vitality.

In the Scriptures the picture portrayed of the Promised Land, to which God tried so hard to lead Israel from Egypt, was that of a "land flowing with milk and honey." Not only is this figurative language but also essentially scientific terminology. In agricultural terms we speak of a "milk flow" and "honey flow." By this we mean the peak season of spring and summer when pastures are at their most productive stages. The livestock that feed on the forage and the bees that visit the blossoms are said to be producing a corresponding "flow" of milk or honey. So a land flowing with milk and honey is a land of rich, green, luxuriant pastures.

And when God spoke of such a land for Israel He also foresaw such an abundant life of joy and victory and contentment for His people.

For the child of God, the Old Testament account of Israel moving from Egypt into the Promised Land is a picture of us moving from sin into the life of overcoming victory. We are promised such a life. It has been provided for us and is made possible by the unrelenting effort of Christ on our behalf.

How He works to clear the life of rocks of stony unbelief. How He tries to tear out the roots of bitterness. He attempts to break up the hard, proud human heart that is set like sun-dried clay. He then sows the seed of His own precious Word, which, if given half a chance to grow, will produce rich crops of contentment and peace. He waters this with the dews and rain of His own presence by the Holy Spirit. He tends and cares and cultivates the life, longing to see it become rich and green and productive.

It is all indicative of the unrelenting energy and industry of an owner who wishes to see his sheep satisfied and well fed. It all denotes my Shepherd's desire to see my best interests served. His concern for my care is beyond my comprehension, really. At best all I can do is to enjoy and revel in what He has brought into effect.

This life of quiet overcoming, of happy repose, of rest in His presence, of confidence in His management is something few Christians ever fully enjoy.

Because of our own perverseness we often prefer to feed on the barren ground of the world around us. I used to marvel how some of my sheep actually chose inferior forage at times.

But the Good Shepherd has supplied green pastures for those who care to move in onto them and there find peace and plenty.

4

"HE LEADS ME BESIDE QUIET WATERS"

Although sheep thrive in dry, semi-arid country, they still require water. They are not like some of the African gazelles which can survive fairly well on the modest amount of moisture found in natural forage.

It will be noticed that here again the key or the clue to where water can be obtained lies with the shepherd. It is he who knows where the best drinking places are. In fact, very often he is the one who with much effort and industry has provided the watering places. And it is to these spots that he leads the flock.

But before thinking about the water sources themselves, we do well to understand the role of water in the animal body and why it is so essential for its well-being. The body of an animal such as a sheep is composed of about 70 percent water on an average. This fluid is used to maintain normal body metabolism; it is a portion of every cell, contributing to its turgidity and normal life functions. Water determines the vitality, strength, and vigor of the sheep and is essential to its health and general well-being.

If the supply of water for an animal drops off, bodily desiccation sets in. This dehydration of the tissues can result in serious damage to them. It can also mean that the animal becomes weak and impoverished.

Any animal is made aware of water lack by thirst. Thirst indicates the need of the body to have its water supply replenished from a source outside itself.

Now, just as the physical body has a capacity and need for water, so Scripture points out to us clearly that the human personality, the human soul, has a capacity and need for the water of the Spirit of the eternal God.

When sheep are thirsty they become restless and set out in search of water. If not led to the good water supplies of clean, pure water, they will often end up drinking from the polluted pot holes where they pick up such internal parasites as nematodes, liver flukes, or other disease germs.

And in precisely the same manner Christ, our Good Shepherd, made it clear that thirsty souls of men and women can only be fully satisfied when their capacity and thirst for spiritual life is fully quenched by drawing on Himself.

In Matthew 5:6 He said, "Blessed are those who hunger and thirst for righteousness, for they will be filled [satisfied]."

At the great feast in Jerusalem He declared boldly, "If anyone is thirsty, let him come to me and drink."

"To drink" in spiritual terminology simply means "to take in" — or "to accept" — or "to believe." That is to say it implies that a person accepts and assimilates the very life of God in Christ to the point where it becomes a part of him.

The difficulty in all of this is that men and women who are "thirsty" for God (who do have a deep inner sense of searching and seeking; who are in quest of that which will completely satisfy) often are unsure of where to look or really what they are looking for. Their inner spiritual capacity for God and divine life is desiccated, and in their dilemma they will drink from any dirty pool to try and satisfy their thirst for fulfillment.

Saint Augustine of Africa summed it up so well when he wrote, "O God! Thou hast made us for Thyself, and our souls are restless, searching, 'til they find their rest in Thee."

All the long and complex history of earth's religions, pagan worship, and human philosophy is bound up with this insatiable thirst for God.

David, when he composed Psalm 23, knew this. Looking at life from the standpoint of a sheep, he wrote, "He [the Good Shepherd] leads me beside quiet waters." In other words, He alone knows where the still, quiet, deep, clean, pure water is to be found that can satisfy His sheep and keep them fit.

Generally speaking, water for the sheep came from three main sources: dew on the grass, deep wells, or springs and streams.

Most people are not aware that sheep can go for months on end, especially if the weather is not too hot, without actually drinking, if there is heavy dew on the grass each morning. Sheep, by habit, rise just before dawn and start to feed. Or if there is bright moonlight they will graze at night. The early hours are when the vegetation is drenched with dew, and sheep can keep fit on the amount of water taken in with their forage when they graze just before and after dawn.

Of course, dew is a clear, clean, pure source of water. And there is no more resplendent picture of still waters than the silver droplets of dew hanging heavy on leaves and grass at break of day.

The good shepherd, the diligent manager, makes sure that his sheep can be out and grazing on this dew-drenched vegetation. If necessary, it will mean he himself has to rise early to be out with his flock. On the home ranch or afield he will see to it that his sheep benefit from this early grazing.

In the Christian life it is of more than passing significance to observe that those who are often the most serene, most confident, and able to cope with life's complexities are those who rise early each day to feed on God's Word. It is in the quiet, early hours of the morning that they are led beside the quiet, still waters where they imbibe the very life of Christ for the day. This is much more than mere figure of speech. It is practical reality. The biographies of the great men and women of God repeatedly point out how the secret of the success in their spiritual life was attributed to the "quiet time" of each morning. There, alone, still, waiting for the Master's voice, one is led gently to the place where, as the old hymn puts it, "The still dews of His Spirit can be dropped into my life and soul."

One comes away from these hours of meditation, reflection, and communion with Christ refreshed in mind and spirit. The thirst is slaked and the heart is quietly satisfied.

In my mind's eye I can see my flock again. The gentleness, stillness, and softness of early morning always found my sheep knee-deep in dew-drenched grass. There they fed heavily and contentedly. As the sun rose and its heat burned the dewdrops from the leaves, the flock would retire to find shade. There, fully satisfied and happily refreshed, they would lie down to rest and ruminate through the day. Nothing pleased me more.

I am confident this is the same reaction in my Master's heart and mind when I meet the day in the same way. He loves to see me contented, quiet, at rest, and relaxed. He delights to know my soul and spirit have been refreshed and satisfied.

But the irony of life, and tragic truth for most Christians, is that this is not so. They often try, instead, to satisfy their thirst by pursuing almost every other sort of substitute. For their minds and intellects they will pursue knowledge, science, academic careers, vociferous reading, or off-beat companions. But they are always left panting and dissatisfied.

Some of my friends have been among the most learned and highly respected scientists and professors in the country. Yet about them there is often a strange yearning, an unsatisfied thirst which all their learning, all their knowledge, all their achievements have not satisfied.

To appease the craving of their souls and emotions, men and women will turn to the arts, to culture, to music, to literary forms, trying to find fulfillment.

And again, so often, these are amongst the most jaded and dejected of people.

Amongst my acquaintances are some outstanding authors and artists. Yet it is significant that to many of them life is a mockery. They have tried drinking deeply from the wells of the world only to turn away unsatisfied—unquenched in their soul's thirst. There are those who, to quench this thirst in their parched lives, have attempted to find refreshment in all sorts of physical pursuits and activities.

They try travel. Or they participate feverishly in sports. They attempt adventures of all sorts or indulge in social activities. They take up hobbies or engage in community efforts. But when all is said and everything has been done, they find themselves facing the same haunting, hollow, empty, unfilled thirst within.

The ancient prophet Jeremiah put it very bluntly when he declared, "My people ... have forsaken me, the spring of living water, and have dug their own cisterns, broken cisterns that cannot hold water" (Jeremiah 2:13).

It is a compelling picture. It is an accurate portrayal of broken lives—of shattered hopes—of barren souls that are dried up and parched and full of the dust of despair.

Among young people, especially the "beat" generation, the recourse to drugs, to alcohol, to sexual adventure in a mad desire to assuage their thirst is classic proof that such sordid indulgences are no substitute for the Spirit of the living God. These poor people are broken cisterns. Their lives are a misery. I have yet to talk to a truly happy "hippie." Their faces show the desperation within.

And amid all this chaos of a confused, sick society, Christ comes quietly as of old and invites us to come to Him. He invites us to follow Him. He invites us to put our confidence in Him. For He it is who best knows how we can be satisfied. He knows that the human heart, the human personality, the human soul with its amazing capacity for God can never be satisfied with a substitute. Only the Spirit and life of Christ Himself will satisfy the thirsting soul.

Now, strange as it may appear on the surface, the deep wells of God from which we may drink are not always necessarily the delightful experiences we may imagine them to be.

I recall so clearly standing under the blazing equatorial sun of Africa and watching the native herds being led to their owner's water wells. Some of these were enormous, hand-hewn caverns cut from the sandstone formation along the sandy rivers. They were like great rooms chiseled out of the rocks with ramps running down to the water trough at the bottom. The herds and flocks were led down into these deep cisterns where cool, clear, clean water awaited them.

But down in the well, stripped naked, was the owner bailing water to satisfy the flock. It was hard, heavy, hot work. Perspiration poured off the body of the bailer, whose skin glistened under the strain and heat of his labor.

As I stood there watching the animals quench their thirst at the still waters I was again immensely impressed by the fact that everything hinged and depended upon the diligence of the owner, the shepherd. Only through his energy, his efforts, his sweat, his strength could the sheep be satisfied.

In the Christian life exactly the same applies. Many of the places we may be led into will appear to us as dark, deep, dangerous, and somewhat disagreeable. But it simply must be remembered that He is there with us in it. He is very much at work in the situation. It is His energy, effort, and strength expended on my behalf that even in this deep, dark place is bound to produce a benefit for me.

It is there that I will discover He only can really satisfy me. It is He who makes sense and purpose and meaning come out of situations which otherwise would be but a mockery to me. Suddenly life starts to have significance. I discover I am the object of His special care and attention. Dignity and direction come into the events of my life, and I see them sorting themselves out into a definite pattern of usefulness. All of this is refreshing, stimulating, invigorating. My thirst for reality in life is assuaged, and I discover that I have found that satisfaction in my Master.

Of course there is always a percentage of perverse people who will refuse to allow God to lead them. They insist on running their own lives and following the dictates of their own wills. They insist they can be masters of their own destinies even if ultimately such destinies are destructive. They don't want to be directed by the Spirit of God—they don't want to be led by Him—they want to walk in their own ways and drink from any old source that they fancy might satisfy their whims.

They remind me very much of a bunch of sheep I watched one day which were being led down to a magnificent mountain stream. The snow-fed waters were flowing pure and clear and crystal clean between lovely banks of trees. But on the way several stubborn ewes and their lambs stopped, instead, to drink from small, dirty, muddy pools beside the trail. The water was filthy and polluted not only with the churned up mud from the passing sheep but even with the manure and urine of previous flocks that had passed that way. Still these stubborn sheep were quite sure it was the best drink obtainable.

The water itself was filthy and unfit for them. Much more, it was obviously contaminated with nematodes and liver fluke eggs that would eventually riddle them with internal parasites and diseases of destructive impact.

People often try this pursuit or that with the casual comment, "So what? I can't see that it's going to do any harm!" Little do they appreciate that often there is a delayed reaction and that considerable time may elapse before the full impact of their misjudgment strikes home. Then suddenly they are in deep trouble and wonder why.

To offset these dangers and guard against them, God invites us to allow ourselves to be led and guided by His own gracious Spirit. Much of the emphasis and teaching of the Pauline Epistles in the New Testament is that the child of God should not end up in difficulty. Galatians 5 and Romans 8 bring this out very clearly.

Jesus' own teaching to His twelve disciples just before His death, given to us in John 14 through 17, points out that the gracious Holy Spirit was to be given to lead us into truth. He would come as a guide and counselor. Always He would lead us into the things of Christ. He would make us see that the life in Christ was the only truly satisfying life. We would discover the delight of having our souls satisfied with His presence. It would be He who would become to us very meat and drink—that at His resurrection, overcoming life was imparted to me by His Spirit each day I would be refreshed and satisfied.

"HE RESTORES
MY SOUL"

*I*n studying this Psalm it must always be remembered that it is a sheep in the Good Shepherd's care who is speaking. It is essentially a Christian's claim of belonging in the family of God. As such he boasts of the benefits of such a relationship.

This being the case, one might well ask, "Why then this statement ... 'He restores my soul'?" Surely it would be assumed that anyone in the Good Shepherd's care could never become so distressed in soul as to need restoration.

But the fact remains that this does happen.

Even David, the author of the Psalm, who was much loved of God, knew what it was to be cast down and dejected. He had tasted defeat in his life and felt the frustration of having fallen under temptation. David was acquainted with the bitterness of feeling hopeless and without strength in himself.

In Psalm 42:11 he cries out, "Why are you downcast, O my soul? Why so disturbed within me? Put your hope in God...."

Now there is an exact parallel to this in caring for sheep. Only those intimately acquainted with sheep and their habits understand the significance of a "cast" sheep or a "cast down" sheep.

This is an old English shepherd's term for a sheep that has turned over on its back and cannot get up again by itself.

A cast sheep is a very pathetic sight. Lying on its back, its feet in the air, it flays away frantically struggling to stand up, without success. Sometimes it will bleat a little for help, but generally it lies there lashing about in frightened frustration.

If the owner does not arrive on the scene within a reasonably short time, the sheep will die. This is but another reason why it is so essential for a careful sheepman to look over his flock every day, counting them to see that all are able to be up and on their feet. If one or two are missing, often the first thought to flash into his mind is, *One of my sheep is cast somewhere. I must go in search and set it on its feet again.*

One particular ewe that I owned in a flock of Cheviots was notorious for being a cast sheep. Every spring when she became heavy in lamb it was not uncommon for her to become cast every second or third day. Only my diligence made it possible for her to survive from one season to the next. One year I had to be away from the ranch for a few days when she was having her problems. So I called my young son aside and told him he would be responsible for her well-being while I was absent. If he managed to keep her on her feet until I came home, he would be well paid for his efforts. Every evening after school he went out to the fields faithfully and set up the old ewe so she could survive. It was quite a task, but she rewarded us with a fine pair of twin lambs that spring.

It is not only the shepherd who keeps a sharp eye for cast sheep, but also the predators. Buzzards, vultures, dogs, coyotes, and cougars all know that a cast sheep is easy prey and death is not far off.

This knowledge that any cast sheep is helpless, close to death, and vulnerable to attack makes the whole problem of cast sheep serious for the manager.

Nothing seems to so arouse his constant care and diligent attention to the flock as the fact that even the largest, fattest, strongest, and sometimes healthiest sheep can become cast and be a casualty. Actually it is often the fat sheep that are the most easily cast.

The way it happens is this. A heavy, fat, or long-fleeced sheep will lie down comfortably in some little hollow or depression in the ground. It may roll on its side slightly to stretch out or relax. Suddenly the center of gravity in the body shifts so that it turns on its back far enough that the feet no longer touch the ground. It may feel a sense of panic and start to paw frantically. Frequently this only makes things worse. It rolls over even further. Now it is quite impossible for it to regain its feet.

As it lies there struggling, gases begin to build up in the rumen. As these expand they tend to retard and cut off blood circulation to extremities of the body, especially the legs. If the weather is very hot and sunny, a cast sheep can die in a few hours. If it is cool and cloudy and rainy, it may survive in this position for several days.

If the cast sheep is a ewe with lambs, of course, it is a multiple loss to the owner. If the lambs are unborn, they perish with her. If they are young and suckling, they become orphans. All of this adds to the seriousness of the situation.

So it will be seen why a sheepman's attention is always alert for this problem.

During my own years as a keeper of sheep, perhaps some of the most poignant memories are wrapped around the commingled anxiety of keeping a count of my flock and repeatedly saving and restoring cast sheep. It is not easy to convey on paper the sense of this ever-present danger. Often I would go out early and merely cast my eye across the sky.

If I saw the black-winged buzzards circling overhead in their long slow spirals, anxiety would grip me. Leaving everything else, I would immediately go out into the rough wild pastures and count the flock to make sure every one was well and fit and able to be on its feet.

This is part of the pageantry and drama depicted for us in the magnificent story of the ninety and nine sheep with one astray. There is the shepherd's deep concern, his agonizing search, his longing to find the missing one, and his delight in restoring it not only to its feet but also to the flock as well as to himself.

Again and again I would spend hours searching for a single sheep that was missing. Then more often than not I would see it at a distance, down on its back, lying helpless. At once I would start to run toward it—hurrying as fast as I could—for every minute was critical.

Within me there was a mingled sense of fear and joy: fear that it might be too late; joy that it was found at all.

As soon as I reached the cast ewe, my first impulse was to pick it up. Tenderly I would roll the sheep over on its side. This would relieve the pressure of gases in the rumen. If she had been down for long, I would have to lift her onto her feet. Then, straddling the sheep with my legs, I would hold her erect, rubbing her limbs to restore the circulation to her legs. This often took quite a little time. When the sheep started to walk again she often just stumbled, staggered, and collapsed in a heap once more.

All the time I worked on the cast sheep I would talk to it gently: "When are you going to learn to stand on your own feet?" "I'm so glad I found you in time—you rascal!"

Little by little the sheep would regain its equilibrium. It would start to walk steadily and surely. By and by it would dash away to rejoin the others, set free from its fears and frustrations, given another chance to live a little longer.

All of this pageantry is conveyed to my heart and mind when I repeat the simple statement, "He restores my soul!"

There is something intensely personal, intensely tender, intensely endearing, yet intensely fraught with danger in the picture. On the one hand there is the sheep so helpless, so utterly immobilized though otherwise strong, healthy, and flourishing; while on the other hand there is the attentive owner quick and ready to come to its rescue—ever patient and tender and helpful.

At this point it is important to point out that similarly in the Christian life there is an exciting and comforting parallel here.

Many people have the idea that when a child of God falls, when he is frustrated and helpless in a spiritual dilemma, God becomes disgusted, fed-up, and even furious with him.

This simply is not so.

One of the great revelations of the heart of God given to us by Christ is that of Himself as our Shepherd. He has the same identical sensations of anxiety, concern, and compassion for cast men and women as I had for cast sheep. This is precisely why He looked on people with such pathos and compassion. It explains His magnanimous dealing with down-and-out individuals for whom even human society had no use. It reveals why He wept over those who spurned His affection. It discloses the depth of His understanding of undone people to whom He came eagerly and quickly, ready to help, to save, to restore.

When I read the life story of Jesus Christ and examine carefully His conduct in coping with human need, I see Him again and again as the Good Shepherd picking up cast sheep. The tenderness, the love, the patience that He used to restore Peter's soul after the terrible tragedy of his temptations is a classic picture of the Christ coming to restore one of His own.

And so He comes quietly, gently, reassuringly to me no matter when or where or how I may be cast down.

In Psalm 56:13 we are given an accurate commentary on this aspect of the Christian's life in these words, "You have delivered me from death and my feet from stumbling, that I may walk before God in the light of life."

We have to be realistic about the life of the child of God and face facts as they really are. Most of us, though we belong to Christ and desire to be under His control and endeavor to allow ourselves to be led by Him, do on some occasions find ourselves cast down.

We discover that often when we are most sure of ourselves we stumble and fall. Sometimes when we appear to be flourishing in our faith we find ourselves in a situation of utter frustration and futility.

Paul in writing to the Christians at Corinth warned them of this danger. "So, if you think you are standing firm, be careful that you don't fall!" (1 Corinthians 10:12).

Admittedly this may appear as one of the paradoxes and enigmas of our spiritual lives. When we examine it carefully, however, we will not find it too difficult to understand.

As with sheep, so with Christians, some basic principles and parallels apply which will help us to grasp the way in which a man or woman can be cast.

There is, first of all, the idea of looking for a soft spot. The sheep that choose the comfortable, soft, rounded hollows in the ground in which to lie down very often become cast. In such a situation it is so easy to roll over on their backs.

In the Christian life there is great danger in always looking for the easy place, the cozy corner, the comfortable position where there is no hardship, no need for endurance, no demand upon self-discipline.

The time when we think "we have it made," so to speak, is actually when we are in mortal danger. There is such a thing as the discipline of poverty and privation which can be self-imposed to do us worlds of good. Jesus suggested this to the rich young man who mistakenly assumed he was in a safe position when in truth he was on the verge of being cast down.

Sometimes if, through self-indulgence, I am unwilling to forfeit or forego the soft life, the easy way, the cozy corner, then the Good Shepherd may well move me to a pasture where things aren't quite so comfortable—not only for my own good but also His benefit as well.

There is the aspect, too, of a sheep simply having too much wool. Often when the fleece becomes very long and heavily matted with mud, manure, burrs, and other debris, it is much easier for a sheep to become cast, literally weighed down with its own wool.

Wool in Scripture depicts the old self-life in the Christian. It is the outward expression of an inner attitude, the assertion of my own desire and hopes and aspirations. It is the area of my life in which and through which I am continually in contact with the world around me. Here is where I find the clinging accumulation of things, of possessions, of worldly ideas beginning to weigh me down, drag me down, hold me down.

It is significant that no high priest was ever allowed to wear wool when he entered the Holy of Holies. This spoke of self, of pride, of personal preference—and God could not tolerate it.

If I wish to go on walking with God and not be forever cast down, this is an aspect of my life which He must deal with drastically.

Whenever I found that a sheep was being cast because it had too long and heavy a fleece, I soon took swift steps to remedy the situation. In short order I would shear it clean and so forestall the danger of having the ewe lose her life. This was not always a pleasant process. Sheep do not really enjoy being sheared, and it represents some hard work for the shepherd, but it must be done.

Actually when it is all over both sheep and owner are relieved. There is no longer the threat of being cast down, while for the sheep there is the pleasure of being set free from a hot, heavy coat. Often the fleece is clogged with filthy manure, mud, burrs, sticks, and ticks. What a relief to be rid of it all!

And similarly in dealing with our old self-life, there will come a day when the Master must take us in hand and apply the keen cutting edge of His Word to our lives. It may be an unpleasant business for a time. No doubt we'll struggle and kick about it. We may get a few cuts and wounds. But what a relief when it is all over. Oh, the pleasure of being set free from ourselves! What a restoration!

The third chief cause of cast sheep is simply that they are too fat. It is a well-known fact that over-fat sheep are neither the most healthy nor the most productive. And certainly it is the fattest that most often are cast. Their weight simply makes it that much harder for them to be agile and nimble on their feet.

Of course, once a sheepman even suspects that his sheep are becoming cast for this reason, he will take long-range steps to correct the problem. He will put the ewes on a more rigorous ration; they will get less grain, and the general condition of the flock will be watched very closely. It is his aim to see that the sheep are strong, sturdy, and energetic, not fat, flabby, and weak.

Turning to the Christian life, we are confronted with the same sort of problem. There are men and women who, because they may have done well in business or in their careers or their homes, feel that they are flourishing and have "arrived." They may have a sense of well-being and self-assurance, which in itself is dangerous. Often when we are most sure of ourselves we are the most prone to fall flat.

In His warning to the church in Revelation 3:17 God points out that though some considered themselves rich and affluent, they were actually in desperate danger. The same point was made by Jesus in His account of the wealthy farmer who intended to build more and bigger barns, but who, in fact, faced utter ruin.

Material success is no measure of spiritual health. Nor is apparent affluence any criteria of real godliness. And it is well for us that the Shepherd of our souls sees through this exterior and takes steps to set things right.

He may well impose on us some sort of "diet" or "discipline" which we may find a bit rough and unpalatable at first. But again we need to reassure ourselves that it is for our own good, because He is fond of us, and for His own reputation as the Good Shepherd.

In Hebrews 12 we read how God chooses to discipline those He loves. At the time it may prove a tough routine. But the deeper truth is that afterward it produces a life of repose and tranquillity free from the fret and frustration of being cast down like a helpless sheep.

The toughness it takes to face life and the formidable reverses which it brings to us can come only through the discipline of endurance and hardship. In His mercy and love our Master makes this a part of our program. It is part of the price of belonging to Him.

We may rest assured that He will never expect us or ask us to face more than we can stand (1 Corinthians 10:13). But what He does expose us to will strengthen and fortify our faith and confidence in His control. If He is the Good Shepherd, we can rest assured that He knows what He is doing. This in and of itself should be sufficient to continually refresh and restore my soul. I know of nothing which so quiets and enlivens my own spiritual life as the knowledge that God knows what He is doing with me!

"HE GUIDES ME
IN PATHS OF
RIGHTEOUSNESS
FOR HIS
NAME'S SAKE"

Sheep are notorious creatures of habit. If left to themselves, they will follow the same trails until they become ruts; graze the same hills until they turn to desert wastes; pollute their own ground until it is corrupt with disease and parasites. Many of the world's finest sheep ranges have been ruined beyond repair by overgrazing, poor management, and indifferent or ignorant sheep owners.

One need only travel through places like Spain, Greece, Mesopotamia, North Africa, and even parts of the western United States and New Zealand or Australia to see the havoc wrought by sheep on the land. Some areas in these countries which were formerly productive grasslands have gradually been reduced to ravaged wastelands. Too many sheep over too many years under poor management have brought nothing but poverty and disaster in their wake.

A commonly held but serious misconception about sheep is that they can just "get along anywhere." The truth is quite the reverse. No other class of livestock requires more careful handling, more detailed direction, than do sheep. No doubt David, as a shepherd himself, had learned this firsthand from tough experience. He knew beyond dispute that if the flock was to flourish and the owner's reputation was to be held in high esteem as a good manager, the sheep had to be constantly under his meticulous control and guidance.

The first sheep farm I purchased as a young man was a piece of derelict land that had been "sheeped to death." An absentee owner had rented the place to a tenant. The latter simply loaded the ranch with sheep then left them pretty much to their own ways. The result was utter desolation. Fields became so overgrazed and impoverished they would grow little but poverty grass. Little sheep trails had deteriorated into great gullies. Erosion on the slopes was rampant, and the whole place was ravaged almost beyond repair.

All of this happened simply because the sheep, instead of being managed and handled with intelligent care, had been left to struggle for themselves—left to go their own way, left to the whims of their own destructive habits.

The consequence of such indifference is that the sheep gnaw the grass to the very ground until even the roots are damaged. I have seen places in Africa where grass roots were pawed out of the soil, leaving utter barrenness behind. Such abuse means loss of fertility and the exposure of the land to all the ravages of erosion.

Because of the behavior of sheep and their preference for certain favored spots, these well-worn areas become quickly infested with parasites of all kinds. In a short time a whole flock can thus become infected with worms, nematodes, and scab. The final upshot is that both land and owner are ruined while the sheep become thin, wasted, and sickly.

The intelligent shepherd is aware of all this. Not only just for the welfare of his sheep and the health of his land, but also for his own sake and reputation as a rancher, he must take the necessary precautions to safeguard against these adverse animal traits. Such habits, in themselves, comprise very serious hazards.

The greatest single safeguard which a shepherd has in handling his flock is to keep them on the move. That is to say, they dare not be left on the same ground too long. They must be shifted from pasture to pasture periodically. This prevents overgrazing of the forage. It also avoids the rutting of trails and erosion of land from overuse. It forestalls the reinfestation of the sheep with internal parasites or disease, since the sheep move off the infested ground before these organisms complete their life cycles.

In a word—there must be a predetermined plan of action, a deliberate, planned rotation from one grazing ground to another in line with right and proper principles of sound management. This is precisely the sort of action and the idea David had in mind when he spoke of being led in paths of righteousness.

In this following of a precise plan of operation lies the secret for healthy flocks and healthy land. Here is the key to successful sheep husbandry. The owner's entire name and reputation depends on how effectively and efficiently he keeps his charges moving onto wholesome, new, fresh forage. The one who directs his flock along this course is sure of success.

Casting my mind's eye back over the years that I kept sheep, no other single aspect of the ranch operations commanded more of my careful attention than this moving of the sheep. It literally dominated all my decisions. Not a day went by but what I would walk over the pasture in which the sheep were feeding to observe the balance between its growth and the grazing pressure upon it. As soon as the point was reached where I felt the maximum benefit for both sheep and land was not being met, the sheep were moved to a fresh field. On the average this meant they were put onto new ground almost every week. In very large measure, the success I enjoyed in sheep ranching must be attributed to this care in managing my flock.

A similar procedure applies to flocks of sheep taken out on summer range in the hills by itinerant herders. They deliberately lead or drive their sheep onto fresh range almost every day. A pattern of grazing is worked out carefully in advance so that the sheep do not feed over the same ground too long or too frequently. Some shepherds set up a base camp and fan out from it in wide circles, like the lobes of a clover leaf, covering new pasturage each day, returning to camp at night.

Coupled with this entire concept of management, there is of course the owner's intimate knowledge of his pastures. He has been all over this ground again and again. He knows its every advantage and every drawback. He knows where his flock will thrive, and he is aware of where the feed is poor. So he acts accordingly.

A point worthy of mention here is that whenever the shepherd opens a gate into a fresh pasture the sheep are filled with excitement. As they go through the gate, even the staid old ewes will often kick up their heels and leap with delight at the prospect of finding fresh feed. How they enjoy being led onto new ground.

Now as we turn to the human aspect of this theme we will be astonished at some of the parallels. As mentioned earlier, it is no mere whim on God's part to call us sheep. Our behavior patterns and life habits are so much like that of sheep it is well nigh embarrassing.

First of all, Scripture points out that most of us are a stiff-necked and stubborn lot. We prefer to follow our own fancies and turn to our own ways. "We all, like sheep, have gone astray, each of us has turned to his own way" (Isaiah 53:6). And this we do deliberately, repeatedly, even to our own disadvantage. There is something almost terrifying about the destructive self-determination of a human being. It is inexorably interlocked with personal pride and self-assertion. We insist we know what is best for us even though the disastrous results may be self-evident.

Just as sheep will blindly, habitually, stupidly follow one another along the same little trails until they become ruts that erode into gigantic gullies, so we humans cling to the same habits that we have seen ruin other lives.

Turning to "my own way" simply means doing what I want. It implies that I feel free to assert my own wishes and carry out my own ideas.

And this I do in spite of every warning.

We read in Proverbs 14:12 and 16:25, "There is a way that seems right to a man, but in the end it leads to death."

In contrast to which Christ the Good Shepherd comes gently and says, "I am the way and the truth and the life. No one comes to the Father except through me" (John 14:6). "I have come that they may have life, and have it to the full" (John 10:10).

The difficult point is that most of us don't want to come. We don't want to follow. We don't want to be led in the paths of righteousness. Somehow it goes against our grain. We actually prefer to turn to our own way even though it may take us straight into trouble.

The stubborn, self-willed, proud, self-sufficient sheep that persists in pursuing its old paths and grazing on its old polluted ground will end up a bag of bones on ruined land. The world we live in is full of such folk. Broken homes, broken hearts, derelict lives, and twisted personalities remind us everywhere of men and women who have gone their own way. We have a sick society struggling to survive on beleaguered land. The greed and selfishness of mankind leave behind a legacy of ruin and remorse.

Amid all this chaos and confusion Christ the Good Shepherd comes and says, "If anyone would come after me, he must deny himself and take up his cross and follow me" (Mark 8:34). But most of us, even as Christians, simply don't want to do this. We don't want to deny ourselves, give up our right to make our own decisions—we don't want to follow; we don't want to be led.

Of course, most of us, if confronted with this charge, would deny it. We would assert vehemently that we are "led of the Lord." We would insist that we would follow wherever He leads. We sing songs to this effect and give mental assent to the idea. But as far as actually being led in paths of righteousness is concerned, precious few of us follow that path.

Actually this is the pivot point on which a Christian either "goes on" with God or at which point he "goes back" from following on.

There are many willful, wayward, indifferent, self-interested Christians who cannot really be classified as followers of Christ. There are relatively few diligent disciples who forsake all to follow the Master.

Jesus never made light of the cost involved in following Him. In fact, He made it painfully clear that it was a rugged life of rigid self-denial. It entailed a whole new set of attitudes. It was not the natural, normal way a person would ordinarily live, and this is what made the price so prohibitive to most people.

In brief, seven fresh attitudes have to be acquired. They are the equivalent of progressive forward movements onto new ground with God. If one follows them, he will discover fresh pasturage; new, abundant life; and increased health, wholesomeness, and holiness in his walk with God. Nothing will please Him more, and most certainly no other activity on our part will or can result in as great a benefit to other lives around us.

1. Instead of loving myself most, I am willing to love Christ best and others more than myself.

Now love in a scriptural sense is not a soft, sentimental emotion. It is a deliberate act of my will. It means that I am willing to lay down my life, lay myself out, pour myself out on behalf of another. This is precisely what God did for us in Christ. "This is how we know what love is: Jesus Christ laid down his life for us" (1 John 3:16).

The moment I deliberately do something definite either for God or others that costs me something, I am expressing love. Love is "selflessness" or "self-sacrifice" in contradistinction to "selfishness." Most of us know little of living like this or being "led" in this right way. But once a person discovers the delight of doing something for others, he has started through the gate being led into one of God's green pastures.

2. Instead of being one of the crowd, I am willing to be singled out, set apart from the gang.

Most of us, like sheep, are pretty gregarious. We want to belong. We don't want to be different in a deep, distinctive way, though we may wish to be different in minor details that appeal to our selfish egos.

But Christ pointed out that only a few would find His way acceptable. And to be marked as one of His would mean a certain amount of criticism and sarcasm from a cynical society. Many of us don't want this. Just as He was a Man of Sorrows and acquainted with grief, so we may be. Instead of adding to the sorrows and sadness of society, we may be called on to help bear some of the burdens of others, to enter into the suffering of others. Are we ready to do this?

3. Instead of insisting on my rights, I am willing to forego them in favor of others.

Basically this is what the Master meant by denying one's self. It is not easy, nor normal, nor natural to do this. Even in the loving atmosphere of the home, self-assertion is pretty evident, and the powerful exercise of individual rights is always apparent.

But the person who is willing to pocket his pride, to take a back seat, to play second fiddle without a feeling of being abused or put upon has gone a long way onto new ground with God.

There is a tremendous emancipation from "self" in this attitude. One is set free from the shackles of personal pride. It's pretty hard to hurt such a person. He who has no sense of self-importance cannot be offended or deflated. Somehow such people enjoy a wholesome outlook of carefree abandon that makes their Christian lives contagious with contentment and gaiety.

4. Instead of being "boss," I am willing to be at the bottom of the heap. Or to use sheep terminology, instead of being "top ram," I'm willing to be a "tail-ender."

When the desire for self-assertion, self-aggrandizement, self-pleasing gives way to the desire for simply pleasing God and others, much of the fret and strain is drained away from daily living.

A hallmark of the serene soul is the absence of "drive," at least "drive" for self-determination. The person who is prepared to put his personal life and personal affairs in the Master's hands for His management and direction has found the place of rest in fresh fields each day. These are the ones who find time and energy to please others.

5. Instead of finding fault with life and always asking "Why?" I am willing to accept every circumstance of life in an attitude of gratitude.

Human beings, being what they are, somehow feel entitled to question the reasons for everything that happens to them. In many instances life itself becomes a continuous criticism and dissection of one's circumstances and acquaintances. We look for someone or something on which to pin the blame for our misfortunes. We are often quick to forget our blessings, slow to forget our misfortunes.

But if one really believes his affairs are in God's hands, every event, no matter whether joyous or tragic, will be taken as part of God's plan. To know beyond doubt that He does all for our welfare is to be led into a wide area of peace and quietness and strength for every situation.

6. Instead of exercising and asserting my will, I am willing to learn to cooperate with His wishes and comply with His will.

It must be noted that all the steps outlined here involve the will. The saints from earliest times have repeatedly pointed out that nine-tenths of religion, of Christianity, of becoming a true follower, a dedicated disciple, lies in the will.

When men or women allow their will to be crossed out, canceling the great I in their decisions, then indeed the Cross has been applied to their lives. This is the meaning of taking up one's cross daily—to go to one's own death—no longer my will in the matter but His will be done.

7. Instead of choosing my own way, I am willing to choose to follow in Christ's way: simply to do what He asks me to do.

This basically is simple, straightforward obedience. It means I just do what He asks me to do. I go where He invites me to go. I say what He instructs me to say. I act and react in the manner He maintains is in my own best interest as well as for His reputation (if I'm His follower).

Most of us possess a formidable amount of factual information on what the Master expects of us. Precious few have either the will, intention, or determination to act on it and comply with His instructions. But the person who decides to do what God asks him has moved onto fresh ground which will do both him and others a world of good. Besides, it will please the Good Shepherd to no end.

God wants us all to move on with Him. He wants us to walk with Him. He wants it not only for our welfare but for the benefit of others as well as His own dear reputation.

Perhaps there are those who think He expects too much of us. Maybe they feel the demands are too drastic. Some may even consider His call impossible to carry out.

It would be if we had to depend on self-determination or self-discipline to succeed. But if we are in earnest about wanting to do His will, and to be led, *He makes this possible* by His own gracious Spirit who is given to those who *obey* (Acts 5:32). For it is He who works in us *both* to *will* and *to do* of His good pleasure (Philippians 2:13).

7

"EVEN THOUGH I WALK THROUGH THE VALLEY . . ."

From a shepherd's point of view this statement marks the halfway stage in the Psalm. It is as though up to this point the sheep has been boasting to its unfortunate neighbor across the fence about the excellent care it received from its owner on the "home" ranch throughout the winter and spring.

Now it turns to address the shepherd directly. The personal pronouns *I* and *You* enter the conversation. It becomes a most intimate discourse of deep affection.

This is natural and normal. The long treks into the high country with their summer range begin here. Left behind are the neglected sheep on the other side of the fence. Their owner knows nothing of the hill country—the mountain meadows to which these sheep will be led. Their summer will be spent in the close companionship and solitary care of the good shepherd.

Both in Palestine and on our western sheep ranches, this division of the year is common practice. Most of the efficient sheepmen endeavor to take their flocks onto distant ranges during summer.

This often entails long "drives." The sheep move along slowly, feeding as they go, gradually working their way up the mountains behind the receding snow. By late summer they are well up on the remote alpine meadows above the timberline.

With the approach of autumn, early snow settles on the highest ridges, relentlessly forcing the flock to withdraw down to lower elevations. Finally, toward the end of the year as fall passes, the sheep are driven home to the ranch headquarters where they will spend the winter. It is this segment of the yearly operations that is described in the last half of the poem.

During this time the flock is entirely alone with the shepherd. They are in intimate contact with him and under his most personal attention day and night. That is why these last verses are couched in such intimate first-person language. And it is well to remember that all of this is done against a dramatic background of wild mountains, rushing rivers, alpine meadows, and high rangelands.

David, the Psalmist, of course knew this type of terrain firsthand. When Samuel was sent of God to anoint him king over Israel, he was not at home with his brothers on the "home" ranch. Instead he was high up on the hills tending his father's flock. They had to send for him to come home. It is no wonder he could write so clearly and concisely of the relationship between a sheep and its owner.

He knew from firsthand experience about all the difficulties and dangers, as well as the delights, of the treks into high country. Again and again he had gone up into the summer range with his sheep. He knew this wild but wonderful country like the palm of his own strong hand. Never did he take his flock where he had not already been before. Always he had gone ahead to look over the country with care.

All the dangers of rampaging rivers in flood, avalanches, rock slides, poisonous plants, the ravages of predators that raid the flock, or the awesome storms of sleet and hail and snow were familiar to him. He had handled his sheep and managed them with care under all these adverse conditions. Nothing took him by surprise. He was fully prepared to safeguard his flock and tend them with skill under every circumstance.

All of this is brought out in the beautiful simplicity of the last verses. Here is a grandeur, a quietness, an assurance that sets the soul at rest.

"I fear no evil, for you are with me"—with me in every situation, in every dark trial, in every dismal disappointment, in every distressing dilemma.

In the Christian life we often speak of wanting "to move onto higher ground with God." How we long to live above the lowlands of life. We want to get beyond the common crowd, to enter a more intimate walk with God. We speak of mountaintop experiences and we envy those who have ascended the heights and entered into this more sublime sort of life.

Often we get an erroneous idea about how this takes place. It is as though we imagined we could be "air lifted" onto higher ground. On the rough trail of the Christian life this is not so. As with ordinary sheep management, so with God's people, one only gains higher ground by climbing up through the valleys.

Every mountain has its valleys. Its sides are scarred by deep ravines and gulches and draws. And the best route to the top is always along these valleys.

Any sheepman familiar with the high country knows this. He leads his flock gently, but persistently, up the paths that wind through the dark valleys. It should be noticed that the verse states, "Even though *I walk through* the valley of the shadow of death." It does not say I die there, or stop there—but rather "I walk through."

It is customary to use this verse as a consolation to those who are passing through the dark valley of death. But even here, for the child of God, death is not an end but merely the door into a higher and more exalted life of intimate contact with Christ. Death is but the dark valley opening out into an eternity of delight with God. It is not something to fear, but an experience through which one passes on the path to a more perfect life.

The Good Shepherd knows this. It is one reason why He has told us, "Surely I am with you always"—yes, even in the valley of death. What a comfort and what a cheer.

I was keenly aware of this consolation when my wife went to "higher ground." For two years we had walked through the dark valley of death watching her beautiful body being destroyed by cancer. As death approached I sat by her bed, her hand in mine. Gently we "passed" through the valley of death. Both of us were quietly aware of Christ's presence. There was no fear—*just a going on to higher ground.*

For those of us who remain on earth, there is still a life to live here and now.

There are still valleys to walk through during our remaining days. These need not be "dead end" streets. The disappointments, the frustrations, the discouragements, the dilemmas, the dark, difficult days, though they be shadowed valleys, need not be disasters. They can be the road to higher ground in our walk with God.

After all, when we pause to think about it a moment, we must realize that even our modern mountain highways follow the valleys to reach the summit of the passes they traverse. Similarly the ways of God lead upward through the valleys of our lives.

Again and again I remind myself, "O God, this seems terribly tough, but I know for a fact that in the end it will prove to be the easiest and gentlest way to get me onto higher ground." Then when I thank him for the difficult things, the dark days, I discover that He is there with me in my distress. At that point my panic, my fear, my misgivings give way to calm and quiet confidence in His care. Somehow, in a serene quiet way I am assured all will turn out well for my best because He is with me in the valley and things are under His control.

To come to this conviction in the Christian life is to have entered into an attitude of quiet acceptance of every adversity. It is to have moved onto higher ground with God. Knowing Him in this new and intimate manner makes life much more bearable than before.

There is a second reason why sheep are taken to the mountaintops by way of the valleys. Not only is this the way of the gentlest grades, but also it is the well-watered route. Here one finds refreshing water all along the way. There are rivers, streams, springs, and quiet pools in the deep defiles.

During the summer months long drives can be hot and tiresome. The flocks experience intense thirst. How glad they are for the frequent watering places along the valley route where they can be refreshed.

I recall one year when an enormous flock of over 10,000 sheep was being taken through our country en route to their summer range. The owners came asking permission to water their sheep at the river that flowed by our ranch. Their thirsty flocks literally ran to the water's edge to quench their burning thirst under the blazing summer sun. Only in our valley was there water for their parched flesh. How glad we were to share the water with them.

As Christians we will sooner or later discover that it is in the valleys of our lives that we find refreshment from God Himself. It is not until we have walked with Him through some very deep troubles that we discover He can lead us to find our refreshment in Him right there in the midst of our difficulty. We are thrilled beyond words when there comes restoration to our souls and spirits from His own gracious Spirit.

During my wife's illness and after her death I could not get over the strength, solace, and serene outlook imparted to me virtually hour after hour by the presence of God's gracious Spirit Himself.

It was as if I was being repeatedly refreshed and restored despite the most desperate circumstances all around me. Unless one has actually gone through such an experience, it may seem difficult to believe. In fact, there are those who claim they could not face such a situation. But for the man or woman who walks with God through these valleys, such real and actual refreshment *is* available.

The corollary to this is that only those who have been through such dark valleys can console, comfort, or encourage others in similar situations. Often we pray or sing the hymn requesting God to make us an inspiration to someone else. We want, instinctively, to be a channel of blessing to other lives. The simple fact is that just as water can only flow in a ditch or channel or valley — so in the Christian's career the life of God can only flow in blessing through the valleys that have been carved and cut into our own lives by excruciating experiences.

For example, the one best able to comfort another in bereavement is the person who himself has lost a loved one. The one who can best minister to a broken heart is one who has known a broken heart.

Most of us do not want valleys in our lives. We shrink from them with a sense of fear and foreboding. Yet in spite of our worst misgivings God can bring great benefit and lasting benediction to others through those valleys. Let us not always try to avoid the dark things, the distressing days. They may well prove to be the way of greatest refreshment to ourselves and those around us.

A third reason why the rancher chooses to take his flock into the high country by way of the valleys is that this is generally where the richest feed and best forage is to be found along the route.

The flock is moved along gently — they are not hurried. The lambs have never been this way before. The shepherd wants to be sure there will not only be water but also the best grazing available for the ewes and their lambs. Generally the choicest meadows are in these valleys along the stream banks. Here the sheep can feed as they move toward the high country.

Naturally these grassy glades are often on the floor of steep-walled canyons and gulches. There may be towering cliffs above them on either side. The valley floor itself may be in dark shadow with the sun seldom reaching the bottom except for a few hours around noon.

The shepherd knows from past experience that predators like coyotes, bears, wolves, or cougars can take cover in these broken cliffs and from their vantage point prey on his flock. He knows these valleys can be subject to sudden storms and flash floods that send walls of water rampaging down the slopes. There could be rock slides, mud or snow avalanches, and a dozen other natural disasters that would destroy or injure his sheep. But in spite of such hazards he also knows that this is still the best way to take his flock to the high country. He spares himself no pains or trouble or time to keep an eye out for any danger that might develop.

One of the most terrible threats is the sudden chilling storms of sleet, rain, and snow that can sweep down through the valleys from the mountain peaks. If sheep become soaked and chilled with a freezing rain, the exposure can kill them in a very short time. They are thin-skinned creatures, easily susceptible to colds, pneumonia, and other respiratory complications.

I recall one storm I went through in the foothills of the Rockies in early summer.

The morning had been bright and clear. Suddenly around noon enormous dark, black, forbidding clouds began to sweep down over the hills from the north. A chilling wind accompanied the approaching storm. The sky grew blacker by the hour. Suddenly in mid afternoon long streamers of rain and sleet began to sweep across the valley. I ran to take shelter in a clump of stunted, wind-blown spruce. The rain soaked me through. As it fell it cooled the whole country. The rain turned to sleet, then to commingled snow and hail. In a short time the whole mountain slope (in mid July!) was white and frozen. Ominous darkness shrouded the whole scene. The sheep sensed the storm approaching. Perhaps the flock would have perished if they had not raced away to find shelter in the steep cliffs at the edge of the canyon.

But in these valleys was where the grass grew best, and it was the route to the high country.

Our Shepherd knows all of this when He leads us through the valleys. He knows where we can find strength and sustenance and gentle grazing despite every threat of disaster about us.

It is a most reassuring and reinforcing experience to the child of God to discover that there is, even in the dark valley, a source of strength and courage to be found in God. It is when he can look back over life and see how the Shepherd's hand has guided and sustained him in the darkest hours that renewed faith is engendered.

I know of nothing which so stimulates my faith in my heavenly Father as to look back and reflect on His faithfulness to me in every crisis and every chilling circumstance of life. Over and over He has proved His care and concern for my welfare. Again and again I have been conscious of the Good Shepherd's guidance through dark days and deep valleys.

All of this multiplies my confidence in Christ. It is this spiritual, as well as emotional and mental, exposure to the storms and adversities of life that puts stamina into my very being. Because He has led me through without fear before, He can do it again, and again, and again. In this knowledge fear fades and tranquillity of heart and mind takes its place.

Let come what may. Storms may break about me, predators may attack, the rivers of reverses may threaten to inundate me. But because He is in the situation with me, I shall not fear.

To live thus is to have taken some very long treks toward the high country of holy, calm, healthy living with God.

Only the Christian who learns to live this way is able to encourage and inspire the weaker ones around him. Too many of us are shaken up, frightened, and panicked by the storms of life. We claim to have confidence in Christ, but when the first dark shadows sweep over us and the path we tread looks gloomy, we go into a deep slump of despair. Sometimes we just feel like lying down to die. This is not as it should be.

The person with a powerful confidence in Christ; the one who has proved by past experience that God is with him in adversity; the one who walks through life's dark valleys without fear, his head held high, is the one who in turn is a tower of strength and a source of inspiration to his companions.

There are going to be some valleys in life for all of us. The Good Shepherd Himself assured us that "in this world you will have trouble. But take heart! I have overcome the world" (John 16:33).

The basic question is not whether we have many or few valleys. It is not whether those valleys are dark or merely dim with shadows. The question is how do I react to them? How do I go through them? How do I cope with the calamities that come my way?

With Christ I face them calmly.

With His gracious Spirit to guide me I face them fearlessly.

I know of a surety that only through them can I possibly travel on to higher ground with God. In this way not only shall I be blessed but in turn I will become a benediction to others around me who may live in fear.

"YOUR ROD AND YOUR STAFF, THEY COMFORT ME"

*W*hen the shepherd is afield with his flock in the high country, it is customary for him to carry a minimum of equipment. This was especially true in olden times where the sheepman did not have the benefit of mechanized equipment to transport camp supplies across the rough country. Even today the so-called "shepherd shacks" or "cabooses" in which the herder spends his lonely summers with the sheep are equipped with only the barest essentials.

But during the hours that he is actually in the field the sheepman carries only a rifle slung over his shoulder and a long slender staff in his hand. There will be a small knapsack in which are packed his lunch, a bottle of water, and perhaps a few simple first-aid remedies for his flock.

In the Middle East the shepherd carries only a rod and staff. Some of my most vivid boyhood recollections are those of watching the African herdsmen shepherding their stock with only a long slender stick and a rough *knob-kerrie* in their hands.

These are the common and universal equipment of the primitive sheepman.

Each shepherd boy, from the time he first starts to tend his father's flock, takes special pride in the selection of a rod and staff exactly suited to his own size and strength. He goes into the bush and selects a young sapling which is dug from the ground. This is carved and whittled down with great care and patience. The enlarged base of the sapling where its trunk joins the roots is shaped into a smooth, rounded head of hard wood. The sapling itself is shaped to exactly fit the owner's hand. After he completes it, the shepherd boy spends hours practicing with this club, learning how to throw it with amazing speed and accuracy. It becomes his main weapon of defense for both himself and his sheep.

I used to watch the native lads having competitions to see who could throw his rod with the greatest accuracy across the greatest distance. The effectiveness of these crude clubs in the hands of skilled shepherds was a thrill to watch. The rod was, in fact, an extension of the owner's right arm. It stood as a symbol of his strength, his power, his authority in any serious situation. The rod was what he relied on to safeguard both himself and his flock in danger. And it was, furthermore, the instrument he used to discipline and correct any wayward sheep that insisted on wandering away.

There is an interesting sidelight on the word "rod" which has crept into the colloquial language of the West. Here the slang term "rod" has been applied to handguns such as pistols and revolvers which were carried by cowboys and other western rangemen. The connotation is exactly the same as that used in this Psalm.

The sheep asserts that the owner's rod, his weapon of power, authority, and defense, is a continuous comfort to him. For with it the manager is able to carry out effective control of his flock in every situation.

It will be recalled how when God called Moses, the desert shepherd, and sent him to deliver Israel out of Egypt from under Pharaoh's bondage, it was his rod that was to demonstrate the power vested in him. It was always through Moses' rod that miracles were made manifest not only to convince Pharaoh of Moses' divine commission, but also to reassure the people of Israel.

The rod speaks, therefore, of the spoken Word, the expressed intent, the extended activity of God's mind and will in dealing with men. It implies the authority of divinity. It carries with it the convicting power and irrefutable impact of *"Thus saith the Lord."*

Just as for the sheep of David's day there was comfort and consolation in seeing the rod in the shepherd's skillful hands, so in our day there is great assurance in our own hearts as we contemplate the power, veracity, and potent authority vested in God's Word. For, in fact, the Scriptures are His rod. They are the extension of His mind and will and intentions to mortal man.

Living as we do in an era when numerous confused voices and strange philosophies are presented to people, it is reassuring to the child of God to turn to the Word of God and know it to be his Shepherd's hand of authority. What a comfort to have this authoritative, clear-cut, powerful instrument under which to conduct ourselves. By it we are kept from confusion amid chaos. This in itself brings into our lives a great sense of quiet serenity which is precisely what the Psalmist meant when he said, "your rod ... comfort[s] me."

There is a second dimension in which the rod is used by the shepherd for the welfare of his sheep— namely that of discipline. If anything, the club is used for this purpose perhaps more than any other.

I could never get over how often, and with what accuracy, the African herders would hurl their knob-kerries at some recalcitrant beast that misbehaved. If the shepherd saw a sheep wandering away on its own, or approaching poisonous weeds, or getting too close to danger of one sort or another, the club would go whistling through the air to send the wayward animal scurrying back to the bunch.

As has been said of the Scriptures so often, "This Book will keep you from sin!" It is the Word of God that comes swiftly to our hearts, that comes with surprising suddenness to correct and reprove us when we go astray. It is the Spirit of the living God, using the living Word, that convicts our conscience of right conduct. In this way we are kept under control by Christ who wants us to walk in the ways of righteousness.

Another interesting use of the rod in the Shepherd's hand was to examine and count the sheep. In the terminology of the Old Testament this was referred to as passing "under the rod" (see Ezekiel 20:37). This meant not only coming under the owner's control and authority, but also to be subject to his most careful, intimate, and firsthand examination. A sheep that passed "under the rod" was one which had been counted and looked over with great care to make sure all was well with it.

Because of their long wool, it is not always easy to detect disease, wounds, or defects in sheep. For example, at a sheep show an inferior animal can be clipped and shaped and shown so as to appear a perfect specimen. But the skilled judge will take his rod and part the sheep's wool to determine the condition of the skin, the cleanliness of the fleece, and the conformation of the body. In plain language, one just does not "pull the wool over his eyes."

In caring for his sheep, the good shepherd, the careful manager, will from time to time make a careful examination of each individual sheep. The picture is a very poignant one. As each animal comes out of the corral and through the gate, it is stopped by the shepherd's outstretched rod. He opens the fleece with the rod; he runs his skillful hands over the body; he feels for any sign of trouble; he examines the sheep with care to see that all is well. This is a most searching process entailing every intimate detail. It is, too, a comfort to the sheep, for only in this way can its hidden problems be laid bare before the shepherd.

This is what was meant in Psalm 139:23–24 when the Psalmist wrote, "Search me, O God, and know my heart; test me and know my anxious thoughts. See if there is any offensive way in me, and lead me in the way everlasting."

If we will allow it, if we will submit to it, God by His Word will search us. There will be no "pulling the wool over His eyes." He will get below the surface, behind the front of our old self-life and expose things that need to be made right.

This is a process from which we need not shrink. It is not something to avoid. It is done in concern and compassion for our welfare. The Great Shepherd of our souls has our own best interests at heart when He so searches us. What a comfort this should be to the child of God, who can trust in God's care.

Wool in Scripture speaks of the self-life, self-will, self-assertion, self-pride. God has to get below this and do a deep work in our wills to right the wrongs which are often bothering us beneath the surface. So often we put on a fine front and brave, bold exterior when really deep down below there needs to be some remedy applied.

Finally, the shepherd's rod is an instrument of protection both for himself and his sheep when they are in danger. It is used both as a defense and a deterrent against anything that would attack.

The skilled shepherd uses his rod to drive off predators like coyotes, wolves, cougars, or stray dogs. Often it is used to beat the brush, discouraging snakes and other creatures from disturbing the flock. In extreme cases, such as David recounted to Saul, the Psalmist no doubt used his rod to attack the lion and the bear that came to raid his flocks.

Once in Kenya photographing elephants, I was being accompanied by a young Masai herder who carried a club in his hand. We came to the crest of a hill from which we could see a herd of elephants in the thick bush below us. To drive them out into the open we decided to dislodge a boulder and roll it down the slope. As we heaved and pushed against the great rock, a cobra, coiled beneath it, suddenly came into view ready to strike.

In a split second the alert shepherd boy lashed out with his club, killing the snake on the spot. The weapon had never left his hand even while we worked on the rock.

"Your rod ... comfort[s] me." In that instant I saw the meaning of this phrase in a new light. It was the rod ever ready in the shepherd's hand that had saved the day for us.

It was the rod of God's Word that Christ, our Good Shepherd, used in His own encounter with that serpent—Satan—during His desert temptation. It is the same Word of God which we can count on again and again to counter the assaults and attacks of Satan. And it matters not whether the guise he assumes is that of a subtle serpent or a roaring lion that desires to destroy us.

There is no substitute for the Scriptures in coping with the complexities of our social order. We live in an evermore involved and difficult milieu. We are part of a world of men and women whose code of conduct is contrary to all that Christ has advocated. To live with such people is to be ever exposed to enormous temptations of all sorts. Some people are very subtle, very smooth, very sophisticated. Others are capable of outright, violent, vituperative attacks against the children of God.

In every situation and under every circumstance there is comfort in the knowledge that God's Word can meet and master the difficulty if we will rely on it.

We turn now to discuss and consider the shepherd's staff. In a sense, that staff, more than any other item of his personal equipment, identifies the shepherd as a shepherd. No one in any other profession carries a shepherd's staff.

It is uniquely an instrument used for the care and management of sheep — and only sheep. It will not do for cattle, horses, or hogs. It is designed, shaped, and adapted especially to the needs of sheep. And it is used only for their benefit.

The staff is essentially a symbol of the concern, the compassion that a shepherd has for his charges. No other single word can better describe its function on behalf of the flock than that it is for their *comfort*.

Whereas the rod conveys the concept of authority, of power, of discipline, of defense against danger, the word "staff" speaks of all that is longsuffering and kind.

The shepherd's staff is normally a long, slender stick, often with a crook or hook on one end. It is selected with care by the owner; it is shaped, smoothed, and cut to best suit his own personal use.

Some of the most moving memories I carry with me from Africa and the Middle East are of seeing elderly shepherds in the twilight of life, standing silently at sunset leaning on their staffs, watching their flocks with contented spirits. Somehow the staff is of special comfort to the shepherd himself. In the tough tramps and during the long weary watches with his sheep he leans on it for support and strength. It becomes to him a most precious comfort and help in his duties.

Just as the rod of God is emblematic of the Word of God, so the staff of God is symbolic of the Spirit of God. In Christ's dealings with us as individuals there is the essence of the sweetness, the comfort and consolation, the gentle correction brought about by the work of His gracious Spirit.

There are three areas of sheep management in which the staff plays a most significant role. The first of these lies in drawing sheep together into an intimate relationship. The shepherd will use his staff to gently lift a newborn lamb and bring it to its mother if they become separated. He does this because he does not wish to have the ewe reject her offspring if it bears the odor of his hands upon it. I have watched skilled shepherds moving swiftly with their staffs amongst thousands of ewes that were lambing simultaneously. With deft but gentle strokes the newborn lambs are lifted with the staff and placed side by side with their dams. It is a touching sight that can hold one spellbound for hours.

But in precisely the same way, the staff is used by the shepherd to reach out and catch individual sheep, young or old, and draw them close to himself for intimate examination. The staff is very useful this way for the shy and timid sheep that normally tend to keep at a distance from the shepherd.

Similarly in the Christian life we find the gracious Holy Spirit, the Comforter, drawing folks together into a warm, personal fellowship with one another. It is also He who draws us to Christ, for as we are told in Revelation, "The Spirit and the bride say, 'Come!'"

The staff is also used for guiding sheep. Again and again I have seen a shepherd use his staff to guide his sheep gently into a new path or through some gate or along dangerous, difficult routes. He does not use it actually to beat the beast. Rather, the tip of the long slender stick is laid gently against the animal's side, and the pressure applied guides the sheep in the way the owner wants it to go. Thus the sheep is reassured of its proper path.

Sometimes I have been fascinated to see how a shepherd will actually hold his staff against the side of some sheep that is a special pet or favorite, simply so that they are "in touch." They will walk along this way almost as though it were "hand-in-hand." The sheep obviously enjoys this special attention from the shepherd and revels in the close, personal, intimate contact between them. To be treated in this special way by the shepherd is to know comfort in a deep dimension. It is a delightful and moving picture.

In our walk with God we are told explicitly by Christ Himself that it would be His Spirit who would be sent to guide us and to lead us into all truth (John 16:13). This same gracious Spirit takes the truth of God, the Word of God, and makes it plain to our hearts and minds and spiritual understanding. It is He who gently, tenderly, but persistently says to us, "This is the way—walk in it." And as we comply and cooperate with His gentle promptings, a sense of safety, comfort, and well-being envelops us.

It is He, too, who comes quietly but emphatically to make the life of Christ, my Shepherd, real and personal and intimate to me. Through Him I am "in touch" with Christ. There steals over me the keen awareness that I am His and He is mine. The gracious Spirit continually brings home to me the acute consciousness that I am God's child and He is my Father. In all of this there is enormous comfort and a sublime sense of "oneness," of "belonging," of "being in His care," and hence the object of His special affection.

The Christian life is not just one of subscribing to certain doctrines or believing certain facts. Essential as all of this confidence in the Scriptures may be, there is, as well, the actual reality of experiencing and knowing firsthand the feel of His touch — the sense of His Spirit upon my spirit. There is for the true child of God that intimate, subtle, yet magnificent experience of sensing the Comforter at his side. This is not imagination — it is the genuine, bona fide reality of everyday life. There is a calm, quiet repose in the knowledge that He is there to direct even in the most minute details of daily living. He can be relied on to assist us in every decision, and in this there lies tremendous comfort for the Christian.

Over and over I have turned to Him and in audible, open language asked for His opinion on a problem. I have asked, "What would you do in this case?" or I have said, "You are here now. You know all the complexities; tell me precisely what is the best procedure at this point." And the thrilling thing is He does just that. He actually conveys the mind of Christ in the matter to my mind. Then the right decisions are made with confidence.

It is when I do not do this that I end up in difficulty. It is then that I find myself in a jam of some sort. And here again the gracious Spirit comes to my rescue just as the shepherd rescues his sheep out of the situations into which their own stupidity leads them.

Being stubborn creatures, sheep often get into the most ridiculous and preposterous dilemmas.

I have seen my own sheep, greedy for one more mouthful of green grass, climb down steep cliffs where they slipped and fell into the sea. Only my long shepherd's staff could lift them out of the water back onto solid ground again. One winter day I spent several hours rescuing a ewe that had done this very thing several times before. Her stubbornness was her undoing.

Another common occurrence was to find sheep stuck fast in labyrinths of wild roses or brambles where they had pushed in to find a few stray mouthfuls of green grass. Soon the thorns were so hooked in their wool they could not possibly pull free, tug as they might. Only the use of a staff could free them from their entanglement.

Likewise with us. Many of our jams and impasses are of our own making. In stubborn, self-willed self-assertion we keep pushing ourselves into a situation where we cannot extricate ourselves. Then in tenderness, compassion, and care our Shepherd comes to us. He draws near and in tenderness lifts us by His Spirit out of the difficulty and dilemma. What patience God has with us! What longsuffering and compassion! What forgiveness!

Your staff comforts me! Your Spirit, O Christ, is my consolation!

"YOU PREPARE A
TABLE BEFORE ME . . ."

*I*n thinking about this statement it is well to bear in mind that the sheep are approaching the high mountain country of the summer ranges. These are known as alplands or tablelands so much sought after by sheepmen.

In some of the finest sheep country in the world, especially in the western United States and southern Europe, the high plateaus of the sheep ranges are always referred to as "mesas"—the Spanish word for "tables."

Oddly enough the Kiswahili (African) word for a table is also "mesa." Presumably this had its origin with the first Portuguese explorers to touch the East

African coast. In fact, the use of this word is not uncommon in referring to the high, flat-topped plateaus of the continent. The classic example, of course, is Table Mountain, near Cape Town, which is world renowned.

So it may be seen that what David referred to as a table was actually the entire high summer range. Though these mesas may have been remote and hard to reach, the energetic and aggressive sheep owner takes the time and trouble to ready them for the arrival of his flocks.

Early in the season, even before all the snow has been melted by spring sunshine, he will go ahead and make preliminary survey trips into this rough, wild country. He will look it over with great care, keeping ever in mind its best use for his flock during the coming season.

Then just before the sheep arrive, he will make another expedition or two to prepare the tableland for them. He takes along a supply of salt and minerals to be distributed over the range at strategic spots for the benefit of the sheep during the summer. The intelligent, careful manager will also decide well ahead of time where his camps will be located so the sheep have the best bed grounds. He goes over the range carefully to determine how vigorous the grass and upland vegetation is. At this time he decides whether some glades and basins can be used only lightly whereas other slopes and meadows may be grazed more heavily.

He will check to see if there are poisonous weeds appearing, and if so, he will plan his grazing program to avoid them or take drastic steps to eradicate them.

Unknown to me, the first sheep ranch I owned had a rather prolific native strand of both blue and white cammas. The blue cammas were a delightful sight in the spring when they bloomed along the beaches. The white cammas, though a much less conspicuous flower, were also quite attractive but a deadly menace to sheep. If lambs, in particular, ate or even just nibbled a few of the lily-like leaves as they emerged in the grass sward during spring, it would spell certain death. The lambs would become paralyzed, stiffen up like blocks of wood, and simply succumb to the toxic poisons from the plants.

My youngsters and I spent days and days going over the ground plucking out these poisonous plants. It was a recurring task that was done every spring before the sheep went on these pastures. Though tedious and tiring with all of the bending, it was a case of "preparing the table in the presence of my enemies." And if my sheep were to survive, it simply had to be done.

A humorous sidelight on this chore was the way I hit on the idea of making up animal stories to occupy the children's minds as we worked together this way for long hours, often down on our hands and knees. They would become so engrossed in my wild fantasies about bears and skunks and raccoons that the hours passed quite quickly. Sometimes both of them would roll in the grass with laughter as I added realistic action to enliven my tales. It was one way to accomplish an otherwise terribly routine task.

All of this sort of thing was in the back of David's mind as he penned these lines. I can picture him walking slowly over the summer range ahead of his flock. His eagle eye is sharp for any signs of poisonous weeds which he would pluck before his sheep got to them. No doubt he had armfuls to get rid of for the safety of his flock.

The parallel in the Christian life is clear. Like sheep, and especially lambs, we somehow feel that we have to try everything that comes our way. We have to taste this thing and that, sampling everything just to see what it's like. And we may very well know that some things are deadly. They can do us no good. They can be most destructive. Still somehow we give them a whirl anyway.

To forestall our getting into grief of this sort, we need to remember our Master has been there ahead of us coping with every situation which would otherwise undo us.

A classic example of this was the incident when Jesus warned Peter that Satan desired to tempt him and sift him like wheat. But Christ pointed out that He had prayed that Peter's faith might not fail during the desperate difficulty he would encounter. And so it is even today. Our great Good Shepherd is going ahead of us in every situation, anticipating what danger we may encounter, and praying for us that in it we might not succumb.

Another task the attentive shepherd takes on in the summer is to keep an eye out for predators. He will look for signs and spoor of wolves, coyotes, cougars, and bears. If these raid or molest the sheep, he will have to hunt them down or go to great pains to trap them so that his flock can rest in peace.

Often what actually happens is that these crafty ones are up on the rimrock watching every movement the sheep make, hoping for a chance to make a swift, sneaking attack that will stampede the sheep. Then one of the flock is bound to fall easy prey to the attacker's fierce teeth and claws.

The picture here is full of drama, action, suspense—and possible death. Only the alertness of the sheepman who tends his flock on the tableland in full view of possible enemies can prevent them from falling prey to attack. It is only his preparation for such an eventuality that can possibly save the sheep from being slaughtered and panicked by their predators.

And again we are given a sublime picture of our Saviour who knows every wile, every trick, every treachery of our enemy Satan and his companions. Always we are in danger of attack. Scripture sometimes refers to him as "a roaring lion" who goes about seeking whom he may devour.

It is rather fashionable in some contemporary Christian circles to discredit Satan. There is a tendency to try and write him off or laugh him off as though he were just a joke. Some deny that such a being as Satan even exists. Yet we see evidence of his merciless attacks and carnage in a society where men and women fall prey to his cunning tactics every day. We see lives torn and marred and seared by his assaults though we may never see him personally.

It reminds me of my encounters with cougars. On several occasions these cunning creatures came in among my sheep at night working terrible havoc in the flock. Some ewes were killed outright, their blood drained and livers eaten. Others were torn open and badly clawed. In these cases the great cats seemed to chase and play with them in their panic like a housecat would chase a mouse. Some had huge patches of wool torn from their fleeces. In their frightened stampede some had stumbled and broken bones or rushed over rough ground injuring legs and bodies.

Yet despite the damage, despite the dead sheep, despite the injuries and fear instilled in the flock, I never once actually saw a cougar on my range. So cunning and so skillful were their raids that they defy description.

At all times we would be wise to walk a little closer to Christ. This is one sure place of safety. It was always the distant sheep, the roamers, the wanderers that were picked off by the predators in an unsuspecting moment. Generally the attackers are gone before the shepherd is alerted by their cry for help. Some sheep, of course, are utterly dumb with fear under attack; they will not even give a plaintive bleat before their blood is spilled.

The same is true of Christians. Many of us get into deep difficulty beyond ourselves; we are stricken dumb with apprehension, unable even to call or cry out for help; we just crumple under our adversary's attack.

But Christ is too concerned about us to allow this to happen. Our Shepherd wants to forestall such a calamity. He wants our mountaintop times to be tranquil interludes. And they will be if we just have the common sense to stay near Him where He can protect us. Read His Word each day. Spend some time talking to Him. We should give Him opportunity to converse with us by His Spirit as we contemplate His life and work for us as our Shepherd.

There is another chore the sheepman takes care of on the tableland. He clears out the water holes, springs, and drinking places for his stock. He has to clean out the accumulated debris of leaves, twigs, stones, and soil that may have fallen into the water source during the autumn and winter. He may need to repair small earth dams he has made to hold water. And he will open the springs that may have become overgrown with grass and brush and weeds. It is all his work, his preparation of the table for his own sheep in summer.

The parallel in the Christian life is that Christ, our great Good Shepherd, has Himself already gone before us into every situation and every extremity that we might encounter. We are told emphatically that He was tempted in all points like as we are. We know He entered fully and completely and very intimately into the life of men upon our planet. He has known our sufferings, experienced our sorrows, and endured our struggles in this life; He was a Man of Sorrows and acquainted with grief.

Because of this He *understands* us; He has totally *identified* Himself with humanity. He has, therefore, a care and compassion for us beyond our ability to grasp. No wonder He makes every possible provision to insure that when we have to cope with Satan, sin, or self, the contest will not be one-sided. Rather, we can be sure He has been in that situation before; He is in it now again with us, and because of this, the prospects of our preservation are excellent.

It is this attitude of rest in Him, of confidence in His care, of relaxation as we realize His presence in the picture that can make the Christian's life one of calm and quiet confidence. The Christian walk can thus become a mountaintop experience—a tableland trip—simply because we are in the care and control of Christ, who has been over all this territory before us and prepared the "table" for us in plain view of our enemies who would demoralize and destroy us if they could.

It is encouraging to know that just as in any other aspect of life where there are lights and shadows, so in the Christian life there are valleys and mountaintops. Too many people assume that once one becomes a Christian, automatically life becomes one glorious garden of delight. This is simply not the case. It may well become a garden of sorrow just as our Saviour went through the garden of Gethsemane. As was pointed out previously, you do not have mountains without valleys, and even on the mountaintop there can be some tough experiences.

Just because the shepherd has gone ahead and made every possible provision for the safety and welfare of his sheep while they are on the summer range does not mean they will not have problems there. Predators can still attack, poisonous weeds can still grow, storms and gales can still come swirling up over the peaks, and a dozen other hazards can haunt the high country.

Yet in His care and concern for us, Christ still insures that we shall have some gladness with our sadness, some delightful days as well as dark days, some sunshine as well as shadow.

It is not always apparent to us what tremendous personal cost it has been for Christ to prepare the table for His own. Just as the lonely, personal privation of the sheepman who prepares the summer range for his stock entails a sacrifice, so the lonely agony of Gethsemane, of Pilate's hall, of Calvary, have cost my Master much.

When I come to the Lord's Table and partake of the communion service which is a feast of thanksgiving for His love and care, do I fully appreciate what it has cost Him to prepare this table for me?

Here we commemorate the greatest and deepest demonstration of *true love* the world has ever known. For God looked down upon sorrowing, struggling, sinning humanity and was moved with compassion for the contrary, sheep-like creatures He had made. In spite of the tremendous personal cost it would entail to deliver them from their dilemma, He chose deliberately to descend and live amongst them that He might deliver them.

This meant laying aside His splendor, His position, His prerogatives as the perfect and faultless One. He knew He would be exposed to terrible privation, to ridicule, to false accusations, to rumor, to gossip, and to malicious charges that branded Him as a glutton, drunkard, friend of sinners, and even an imposter. It entailed losing His reputation. It would involve physical suffering, mental anguish, and spiritual agony.

In short, His coming to earth as the Christ, as Jesus of Nazareth, was a straightforward case of utter self-sacrifice that culminated in the cross of Calvary. The laid-down life, the poured-out blood were the supreme symbols of total selflessness. This was *love*. This was *God*. This was *divinity* in action, delivering men from their own utter selfishness, their own stupidity, their own suicidal instincts as lost sheep unable to help themselves.

In all of this there is an amazing mystery. No man will ever be able fully to fathom its implications. It is bound up inexorably with the concept of God's divine love of self-sacrifice which is so foreign to most of us who are so self-centered. At best we can only grasp feebly the incredible concept of a perfect person, a sinless one being willing actually to be made sin that we who are so full of faults, selfish self-assertion, and suspicion might be set free from sin and self to live a new, free, fresh, abundant life of righteousness.

Jesus told us Himself that He had come that we might have life and have it more abundantly. Just as the sheepman is thrilled beyond words to see his sheep thriving on the high, rich summer range (it is one of the highlights of his whole year), so my Shepherd is immensely pleased when He sees me flourish on the tablelands of a noble, lofty life that He has made possible for me.

Part of the mystery and wonder of Calvary, of God's love to us in Christ, is bound up too with the deep desire of His heart to have me live on a higher plane. He longs to see me living above the mundane level of common humanity. He is so pleased when I walk in the ways of holiness, of selflessness, of serene contentment in His care, aware of His presence and enjoying the intimacy of His companionship.

To live thus is to live richly.

To walk here is to walk with quiet assurance.

To feed here is to be replete with good things.

To find this tableland is to have found something of my Shepherd's love for me.

"YOU ANOINT MY
HEAD WITH OIL . . ."

*A*s one meditates on this magnificent poem it is helpful to keep in mind that the poet is recounting the salient events of the full year in a sheep's life. He takes us with him from the home ranch where every need is so carefully supplied by the owner, out into the green pastures, along the still waters, up through the mountain valleys to the high tablelands of summer.

Here, now, where it would appear the sheep are in a sublime setting on the high meadows, where there are clear running springs, where the forage is fresh and tender, where there is the intimate contact with the shepherd, suddenly we find "a fly in the ointment," so to speak.

For in the terminology of the sheepman, "summertime is fly time." By this, reference is made to the hordes of insects that emerge with the advent of warm weather. Only those people who have kept livestock or studied wildlife habits are aware of the serious problems for animals presented by insects in the summer.

To name just a few parasites that trouble stock and make their lives a misery: there are warble flies, bot flies, heel flies, nose (nasal) flies, deer flies, black flies, mosquitoes, gnats, and other minute, winged parasites that proliferate at this time of year. Their attacks on animals can readily turn the golden summer months into a time of torture for sheep and drive them almost to distraction.

Sheep are especially troubled by the nose fly, or nasal fly, as it is sometimes called. These little flies buzz about the sheep's head, attempting to deposit their eggs on the damp mucous membranes of the sheep's nose. If they are successful, the eggs will hatch in a few days to form small, slender, worm-like larvae. They work their way up the nasal passages into the sheep's head; they burrow into the flesh and there set up an intense irritation accompanied by severe inflammation.

For relief from this agonizing annoyance sheep will deliberately beat their heads against trees, rocks, posts, or brush. They will rub them in the soil and thrash around against woody growth. In extreme cases of intense infestation a sheep may even kill itself in a frenzied endeavor to gain respite from the aggravation. Often advanced stages of infection from these flies will lead to blindness.

Because of all this, when the nose flies hover around the flock, some of the sheep become frantic with fear and panic in their attempt to escape their tormentors. They will stamp their feet erratically and race from place to place in the pasture trying desperately to elude the flies. Some may run so much they will drop from sheer exhaustion. Others may toss their heads up and down for hours.

They will hide in any bush or woodland that offers shelter. On some occasions they may refuse to graze in the open at all.

All this excitement and distraction has a devastating effect on the entire flock.

Ewes and lambs rapidly lose condition and begin to drop in weight. The ewes will go off milking, and their lambs will stop growing gainfully. Some sheep will be injured in their headlong rushes of panic; others may be blinded and some even killed outright.

Only the strictest attention to the behavior of the sheep by the shepherd can forestall the difficulties of "fly time." At the very first sign of flies among the flock he will apply an antidote to their heads. I always preferred to use a homemade remedy composed of linseed oil, sulfur, and tar, which was smeared over the sheep's nose and head as a protection against nose flies.

What an incredible transformation this would make among the sheep. Once the oil had been applied to the sheep's head, there was an immediate change in behavior. Gone was the aggravation, gone the frenzy, gone the irritability and the restlessness. Instead, the sheep would start to feed quietly again, then soon lie down in peaceful contentment.

This, to me, is the exact picture of irritations in my own life. How easy it is for there to be a fly in the ointment of even my most lofty spiritual experience! So often it is the small, petty annoyances that ruin my repose. It is the niggling distractions that become burning issues that can well-nigh drive me round the bend or up the wall. At times some tiny, tantalizing thing torments me to the point where I feel I am just beating my brains out.

And so my behavior as a child of God degenerates to a most disgraceful sort of frustrated tirade.

Just as with the sheep, there must be continuous and renewed application of oil to forestall the "flies" in my life; there must be a continuous anointing of God's gracious Spirit to counteract the ever-present aggravations of personality conflicts. Only one application of oil, sulfur, and tar was not enough for the entire summer. It was a process that had to be repeated. The fresh application was the effective antidote.

There are those who contend that in the Christian life one need only have a single, initial anointing of God's Spirit. Yet the frustrations of daily dilemmas demonstrate that one must have Him come continuously to the troubled mind and heart to counteract the attacks of one's tormentors.

This is a practical and intimate matter between myself and my Master. In Luke 11:13 Christ Himself, our Shepherd, urges us to ask for the Holy Spirit to be given to us by the Father.

It is both a logical and legitimate desire for us to have the daily anointing of God's gracious Spirit upon our minds. God alone can form in us the mind of Christ. The Holy Spirit alone can give to us the attitudes of Christ. He alone makes it possible for us to react to aggravations and annoyances with quietness and calmness.

When people or circumstances or events beyond our control tend to "bug" us, it is possible to be content and serene when these "outside" forces are counteracted by the presence of God's Spirit. In Romans 8:1–2, we are told plainly that it is the law of the Spirit of life in Christ Jesus that makes us free from the law of sin and death.

It is this daily anointing of God's gracious Spirit upon my mind which produces in my life such personality traits as joy, contentment, love, patience, gentleness, and peace. What a contrast this is to the tempers, frustration, and irritableness which mar the daily conduct of so many of God's children.

What I do in any given situation is to expose it to my Master, my Owner, Christ Jesus, and say simply, "O Lord, I can't cope with these petty, annoying, peevish problems. Please apply the oil of Your Spirit to my mind. Both at the conscious and subconscious levels of my thought-life enable me to act and react just as You would." And He will. It will surprise you how promptly He complies with such a request made in deadly earnest.

But summertime for the sheep is more than just fly time. It is also "scab time." Scab is an irritating and highly contagious disease common among sheep the world over. Caused by a minute, microscopic parasite that proliferates in warm weather, "scab" spreads throughout a flock by direct contact between infected and noninfected animals.

Sheep love to rub heads in an affectionate and friendly manner. Scab is most commonly found around the head. When two sheep rub together, the infection spreads readily from one to the other.

In the Old Testament when it was declared that the sacrificial lambs should be without blemish, the thought uppermost in the writer's mind was that the animal should be free of scab. In a very real and direct sense scab is significant of contamination, of sin, of evil.

Again as with flies, the only effective antidote is to apply linseed oil, sulfur, and other chemicals that can control this disease. In many sheep-rearing countries dips are built and the entire flock is put through the dip. Each animal is completely submerged in the solution until its entire body is soaked. The most difficult part to do is the head. The head has to be plunged under repeatedly to insure that scab there will be controlled. Some sheepmen take great care to treat the head by hand.

Only once did my sheep become infected by scab. I had purchased a few extra ewes from another rancher to increase the flock. It so happened they had, unknown to me, a slight infection of scab which quickly began to spread through the entire healthy flock. It meant I had to purchase a huge dipping tank and install it in my corrals. At great expense, to say nothing of the time and heavy labor involved, I had to put the entire flock, one by one, through the dipping solution to clear them of the disease. It was a tremendous task and one that entailed special attention to their heads. So I know precisely what David meant when he wrote, "You anoint my head with oil." Again it was the only antidote for scab.

Perhaps it should be mentioned that in Palestine the old remedy for this disease was olive oil mixed with sulfur and spices. This home remedy served equally well in the case of flies that came to annoy the flocks.

In the Christian life, most of our contamination by the world, by sin, by that which would defile and disease us spiritually comes through our minds. It is a case of mind meeting mind to transmit ideas, concepts, and attitudes that may be damaging.

Often it is when we "get our heads together" with someone else who may not necessarily have the mind of Christ that we come away imbued with concepts that are not Christian.

Our thoughts, our ideas, our emotions, our choices, our impulses, drives, and desires are all shaped and molded through the exposure of our minds to other people's minds. In our modern era of mass communication, the danger of the "mass mind" grows increasingly grave. Young people in particular, whose minds are so malleable, find themselves being molded under the subtle pressures and impacts made on them by television, radio, magazines, newspapers, and fellow classmates, to say nothing of their parents and teachers.

Often the mass media that are largely responsible for shaping our minds are in the control of men whose character is not Christlike, who in some cases are actually anti-Christian.

One cannot be exposed to such contacts without coming away contaminated. The thought patterns of people are becoming increasingly abhorrent. Today we find more tendency to violence, hatred, prejudice, greed, cynicism, and increasing disrespect for that which is noble, fine, pure, or beautiful.

This is precisely the opposite of what Scripture teaches us. In Philippians 4:8 we are instructed emphatically in this matter, " ... whatever is true, whatever is noble, whatever is right, whatever is pure, whatever is lovely, whatever is admirable— if anything is excellent or praiseworthy—think about such things"! Here again, the only possible, practical path to attaining such a mind free of the world's contamination is to be conscious daily, hourly of the purging presence of God's Holy Spirit, applying Him to my mind.

There are those who seem unable to realize His control of their minds and thoughts. It is a simple matter of faith and acceptance. Just as one asks Christ to come into the life initially to assure complete control of one's conduct, so one invites the Holy Spirit to come into one's conscious and subconscious mind to monitor one's thought-life. Just as by faith we believe and know and accept and thank Christ for coming into our lives, so by simple faith and confidence in the same Christ, we believe and know and accept with thanks the coming (or anointing) of His gracious Spirit upon our minds. Then having done this, we simply proceed to live and act and think as He directs us.

The difficulty is that some of us are not in dead earnest about it. Like a stubborn sheep we will struggle, kick, and protest when the Master puts His hand upon us for this purpose. Even if it is for our own good, we still rebel and refuse to have Him help us when we need it so desperately.

In a sense we are a stiff-necked lot, and were it not for Christ's continuing compassion and concern for us, most of us would be beyond hope or help. Sometimes I am quite sure Christ comes to us and applies the oil of His own Spirit to our minds in spite of our own objections. Were this not so, where would most of us be? Surely every gracious thought that enters my mind had its origin in Him.

Now as summer in the high country moves gradually into autumn, subtle changes occur both in the countryside and in the sheep. The nights become cooler; there are the first touches of frost; the insects begin to disappear and are less a pest; the foliage on the hills turns to crimson, gold, and bronze; mist and rain begin to fall; and the earth prepares for winter.

In the flock there are also subtle changes. This is the season of the rut, of mating, of great battles between the rams for possession of the ewes. The necks of the monarchs swell and grow strong. They strut proudly across the pastures and fight furiously for the favors of the ewes. The crash of heads and thud of colliding bodies can be heard through the hours of day and night.

The shepherd knows all about this. He knows that some of the sheep can and will actually kill, injure, and maim each other in these deadly combats. So he decides on a very simple remedy. At this season of the year he will catch his rams and smear their heads with grease. I used to apply generous quantities of axle grease to the head and nose of each ram. Then when they collided in their great crashing battles, the lubricant would make them glance off each other in such a ludicrous way that they stood there feeling rather stupid and frustrated. In this way much of the heat and tension was dissipated and little damage done.

Among God's people there is a considerable amount of knocking each other. Somehow if we don't see eye to eye with the other person, we persist in trying to assert ourselves and become "top sheep." A good many become badly bruised and hurt this way.

In fact, I found as a pastor that much of the grief, the wounds, the hurts, the ill will, the unforgiven things in people's lives could usually be traced back to old rivalries or jealousies or battles that had broken out between believers. Scores of skeptical souls will never enter a church simply because way back in their experience someone had battered them badly.

To forestall and prevent this sort of thing from happening among His people, our Shepherd loves to apply the precious ointment of the presence of His gracious Spirit to our lives. It will be recalled that just before His crucifixion, our Lord, in dealing with His twelve disciples, who even then were caught up in jealous bickering and rivalry for prestige, told of the coming of the Comforter — the Spirit of Truth. Because of His being sent to them, He said, they would know peace. He went on to say that His people would be known everywhere for their love for one another.

But too often this simply is not true among God's own people. They hammer and knock each other, stiff-necked with pride and self-assertion. They are intolerant, dogmatic, and uncharitable with other Christians.

Yet when the gracious Holy Spirit invades a man or woman, when He enters that life and is in control of the personality, the attributes of peace, joy, longsuffering, and generosity become apparent. It is then that suddenly one becomes aware of how ridiculous are all the petty jealousies, rivalries, and animosities that formerly motivated their absurd assertions. This is to come to a place of great contentment in the Shepherd's care. And it is then that the cup of contentment becomes real in the life. As the children of God, the sheep in the Divine Shepherd's care, we should be known as the most contented people on earth. A quiet, restful contentment should be the hallmark of those who call Christ their Master.

If He is the One who has all knowledge and wisdom and understanding of my affairs and management; if He is able to cope with every situation, good or bad, that I encounter, then surely I should be satisfied with His care. In a wonderful way my cup, or my lot in life, is a happy one that overflows with benefits of all sorts.

The trouble is that most of us just don't see it this way. Especially when troubles or disappointments come along, we are apt to feel forgotten by our Shepherd. We act as though He had fallen down on the job.

Actually He is never asleep. He is never lax or careless. He is never indifferent to our well-being. Our Shepherd always has our best interests in mind.

Because of this, we are actually under obligation to be a thankful, grateful, appreciative people. The New Testament instructs us clearly to grasp the idea that the cup of our life is full and overflowing with good, with the life of Christ Himself, and with the presence of His gracious Spirit. And because of this, we should be joyous, grateful, and serene.

This is the overcoming Christian life. It is the life in which a Christian can be content with whatever comes his way (Hebrews 13:5) — *even trouble.* Most of us are glad when things go well. How many of us can give thanks and praise when things go wrong?

Looking again at the round of the year through which the sheep pass in the shepherd's care, we see summer moving into autumn. Storms of sleet and hail and early snow begin to sweep over the high country. Soon the flocks will be driven from the alplands and tablelands. They will turn again toward the home ranch for the long, quiet winter season.

These autumn days can be golden under Indian summer weather. The sheep have respite now from flies and insects and scab. No other season finds them so fit and well and strong. No wonder David wrote, "my cup overflows."

But at the same time, unexpected blizzards can blow up or sleet storms suddenly shroud the hills. The flock and their owner can pass through appalling suffering together.

It is here that I grasp another aspect altogether of the meaning of a cup that overflows. There is in every life a cup of suffering. Jesus Christ referred to His agony in the garden of Gethsemane and at Calvary as His cup. And had it not overflowed with His life poured out for men, we would have perished.

In tending my sheep I carried a bottle in my pocket containing a mixture of brandy and water. Whenever a ewe or lamb was chilled from undue exposure to wet, cold weather I would pour a few spoonfuls down its throat. In a matter of minutes the chilled creature would be on its feet and full of renewed energy. It was especially cute the way the lambs would wiggle their tails with joyous excitement as the warmth from the brandy spread through their bodies.

The important thing was for me to be there on time, to find the frozen, chilled sheep before it was too late. I had to be in the storm with them, alert to every one that was in distress. Some of the most vivid memories of my sheep ranching days are wrapped around the awful storms my flock and I went through together. I can see again the gray-black banks of storm clouds sweeping in off the sea; I can see the sleet and hail and snow sweeping across the hills; I can see the sheep racing for shelter in the tall timber; I can see them standing there soaked, chilled, and dejected. Especially the young lambs went through appalling misery without the benefit of a full, heavy fleece to protect them. Some would succumb and lie down in distress only to become more cramped and chilled.

Then it was that my mixture of brandy and water came to their rescue. I'm sure the Palestine shepherds must have likewise shared their wine with their chilled and frozen sheep.

What a picture of my Master, sharing the wine, the very life blood of His own suffering from His overflowing cup, poured out at Calvary for me. He is there with me in every storm. My Shepherd is alert to every approaching disaster that threatens His people. He has been through the storms of suffering before. He bore our sorrows and was acquainted with our grief.

And now no matter what storms I face, His very life and strength and vitality is poured into mine. It overflows so the cup of my life runs over with His life ... often with great blessing and benefit to others who see me stand up so well in the midst of trials and suffering.

"SURELY GOODNESS AND LOVE WILL FOLLOW ME . . ."

Throughout the study of this Psalm continuous emphasis has been put upon the care exercised by the attentive sheepman. It has been stressed how essential to the welfare of the sheep is the rancher's diligent effort and labor. All the benefits enjoyed by a flock under skilled and loving management have been drawn in bold lines.

Now all of this is summed up here by the Psalmist in one brave but simple statement: "Surely goodness and love will follow me all the days of my life"!

The sheep with such a shepherd knows of a surety that his is a privileged position. No matter what comes, at least and always he can be perfectly sure that goodness and mercy will be in the picture. He reassures himself that he is ever under sound, sympathetic, intelligent ownership. What more need he care about? Goodness and mercy will be the treatment he receives from his master's expert, loving hands.

Not only is this a bold statement, but it is somewhat of a boast, an exclamation of implicit confidence in the One who controls his career and destiny.

How many Christians actually feel this way about Christ? How many of us are truly concerned that no matter what occurs in our lives we are being followed by goodness and mercy? Of course it is very simple to speak this way when things are going well. If my health is excellent, my income is flourishing, my family is well, and my friends are fond of me, it is not hard to say, "Surely goodness and love will follow me all the days of my life."

But what about when one's body breaks down? What do I say when I stand by helpless, as I have had to do, and watch a life partner die by degrees under appalling pain? What is my reaction when my job folds up and there is no money to meet bills? What happens if my children can't make their grades in school or get caught running with the wrong gang? What do I say when suddenly, without good grounds, friends prove false and turn against me?

These are the sort of times that test a person's confidence in the care of Christ. These are the occasions during which the chips are down and life is more than a list of pious platitudes. When my little world is falling apart and the dream castles of my ambitions and hopes crumble into ruins, can I honestly declare, "Surely—yes—surely—goodness and love will follow me all the days of my life"? Or is this sheer humbug and a maddening mockery?

In looking back over my own life, in the light of my love and care for my sheep, I can see again and again a similar compassion and concern for me in my Master's management of my affairs. There were events which at the time seemed like utter calamities; there were paths down which He led me that appeared like blind alleys; there were days He took me through which were well nigh black as night itself. But all in the end turned out for my benefit and my well-being.

With my limited understanding as a finite human being I could not always comprehend His management executed in infinite wisdom. With my natural tendencies to fear, worry, and ask "why," it was not always simple to assume that He really did know what He was doing with me. There were times I was tempted to panic, to bolt, and to leave His care. Somehow I had the strange, stupid notion I could survive better on my own. Most men and women do.

But despite this perverse behavior I am so glad He did not give up. I am so grateful He did follow me in goodness and mercy. The only possible motivation was His own love, His care and concern for me as one of His sheep. And despite my doubts, despite my misgivings about His management of my affairs, He has picked me up and borne me back again in great tenderness.

As I see all of this in retrospect I realize that for the one who is truly in Christ's care, no difficulty can arise, no dilemma emerge, no seeming disaster descend on the life without eventual good coming out of the chaos. This is to see the goodness and mercy of my Master in my life. It has become the great foundation of my faith and confidence in Him.

I love Him because He first loved me.

His goodness and mercy and compassion to me are new every day. And my assurance is lodged in these aspects of His character.

My trust is in His love for me as His own.

My serenity has as its basis an implicit, unshakable reliance on His ability to do the right thing, the best thing in any given situation.

This to me is the *supreme* portrait of my Shepherd. Continually there flows out to me His goodness and His mercy, which, even though I do not deserve them, come unremittingly from their source of supply—His own great heart of love.

Herein is the essence of all that has gone before in this Psalm.

All the care, all the work, all the alert watchfulness, all the skill, all the concern, all the self-sacrifice are born of His love — the love of One who loves His sheep, loves His work, loves His role as a Shepherd.

"I am the good shepherd. The good shepherd lays down his life for the sheep."

"This is how we know what love is: Jesus Christ laid down his life for us" (1 John 3:16).

With all this in view it is then proper to ask myself, "Is this outflow of goodness and mercy for me to stop and stagnate in my life? Is there no way in which it can pass on through me to benefit others?"

Yes, there is a way.

And this aspect is one that eludes many of us.

There is a positive, practical aspect in which my life in turn should be one whereby goodness and mercy follow in my footsteps for the well-being of others.

Just as God's goodness and mercy flow to me all the days of my life, so goodness and mercy should follow me, should be left behind me as a legacy to others wherever I may go.

It is worth reiterating at this point that sheep can, under mismanagement, be the most destructive livestock. In short order they can ruin and ravage land almost beyond remedy. But in bold contrast they can, on the other hand, be the most beneficial of all livestock if properly managed.

Their manure is the best balanced of any produced by domestic stock. When scattered efficiently over the pastures it proves of enormous benefit to the soil. The sheep's habit of seeking the highest rise of ground on which to rest insures that the fertility from the rich lowland is redeposited on the less productive higher ground. No other livestock will consume as wide a variety of herbage. Sheep eat all sorts of weeds and other undesirable plants that might otherwise invade a field. For example, they love the buds and tender tips of Canada thistle, which, if not controlled, can quickly become a most noxious weed. In a few years a flock of well-managed sheep will clean up and restore a piece of ravaged land as no other creature can do.

In ancient literature sheep were referred to as "those of the golden hooves" — simply because they were regarded and esteemed so highly for their beneficial effect on the land.

In my own experience as a sheep rancher, I have, in just a few years, seen two derelict ranches restored to high productivity and usefulness. More than this, what before appeared as depressing eyesores became beautiful, park-like properties of immense worth. Where previously there had been only poverty and pathetic waste, there now followed flourishing fields and rich abundance.

In other words, goodness and mercy had followed my flocks. They left behind them something worthwhile, productive, beautiful, and beneficial to both themselves, others, and me. Where they had walked there followed fertility and weed-free land. Where they had lived there remained beauty and abundance.

The question now comes to me pointedly: Is this true of my life? Do I leave a blessing and benediction behind me?

Sir Alfred Tennyson wrote in one of his great classic poems, "The good men do lives after them."

On one occasion two friends spent a few days in our home while passing through en route to some engagements in the East. They invited me to go along. After several days on the road one of the men missed his hat. He was sure it had been left in our home. He asked me to write my wife to find it and kindly send it on to him.

Her letter of reply was one I shall never forget. One sentence in particular made an enormous impact on me. "I have combed the house from top to bottom and can find no trace of the hat. The only thing those men left behind was a great blessing!"

Is this the way people feel about me?

Do I leave a trail of sadness or of gladness behind?

Is my memory, in other people's minds, entwined with mercy and goodness, or would they rather forget me altogether?

Do I deposit a blessing behind me, or am I a bane to others? Is my life a pleasure to people or a pain?

In Isaiah 52:7 we read, "How beautiful on the mountains are the feet of those who bring good news, who proclaim peace...."

Sometimes it is profitable to ask ourselves such simple questions as:

"Do I leave behind peace in lives—or turmoil?"

"Do I leave behind forgiveness—or bitterness?"

"Do I leave behind contentment—or conflict?"

"Do I leave behind flowers of joy—or frustration?"

"Do I leave behind love—or rancor?"

Some people leave such a sorry mess behind them wherever they go that they prefer to cover their tracks.

For the true child of God, the one under the Shepherd's care, there should never be any sense of shame or fear in going back to where they have lived or been before. Why? Because there they have left a legacy of uplift, encouragement, and inspiration to others.

In Africa, where I spent so many years, one of the greatest marks left by any man was that of David Livingstone. No matter where his footsteps took him through the bush and plains of the great continent, there remained the impact of his love. Natives, whose language he never learned, long years after, remembered him as the kindly, tender doctor whom goodness and mercy had followed all the days of his life.

There remains in my own mind boyhood recollections of the first stories I was told about Jesus Christ as a man amongst us. His life was summed up in the simple, terse, but deeply profound statement, "He went about, doing good!" It was as though this was the loftiest, noblest, most important thing on which He could possibly spend His few short years.

But I also was deeply impressed by the fact that His good and kindly acts were always commingled with mercy. Where so often other human beings were rude and harsh and vindictive of one another, His compassion and tenderness were always apparent. Even the most flagrant sinners found forgiveness with Him, whereas at the hands of their fellow men they knew only condemnation, censure, and cruel criticism.

And again I have to ask myself: Is this my attitude to other people? Do I sit up on my pedestal of self-pride and look with contempt upon my contemporaries, or do I get down and identify myself with them in their dilemma and there extend a small measure of the goodness and mercy given to me by my Master?

Do I see sinners with the compassion of Christ or with the critical eye of censure?

Am I willing to overlook faults and weaknesses in others and extend forgiveness as God has forgiven me my failings?

The only real, practical measure of my appreciation for the goodness and mercy of God to me is the extent to which I am, in turn, prepared to show goodness and mercy to others.

If I am unable to forgive and extend friendship to fallen men and women, then it is quite certain I know little or nothing in a practical sense of Christ's forgiveness and mercy to me.

It is this lack of love among Christians which today makes the church an insipid, lukewarm institution. People come to find affection and are turned off by our tepidity.

But men and women who know firsthand about the goodness and mercy of God in their own lives will be warm and affectionate with goodness and mercy to others. This is to be a benefit to them, but equally important, it is to be a blessing to God.

Yes, a blessing to God!

Most of us think only God can bring a blessing to us. The Christian life is a two-way proposition.

Nothing pleased me more than to see my flock flourish and prosper. It delighted *me* personally to no end to feel compensated for the care I had given them. To see them content was wonderful.

To see the land benefiting was beautiful. And the two together made me a happy man. It enriched my own life; it was a reward for my efforts and energy. In this experience I received full compensation for all that I had poured into the endeavor.

Most of us forget that our Shepherd is looking for some satisfaction as well. We are told that He looked upon the travail of His soul and was satisfied.

This is the benefit we can bring to Him.

He looks on my life in tenderness, for He loves me deeply. He sees the long years during which His goodness and mercy have followed me without slackening. He longs to see some measure of that same goodness and mercy not only passed on to others by me but also passed back to Him with joy.

He longs for love — my love.

And I love Him — only and because He first loved me.

Then He is satisfied.

"I WILL DWELL IN
THE HOUSE OF THE
LORD FOREVER"

This Psalm opened with the proud, joyous statement, "The Lord is my shepherd."

Now it closes with the equally positive, buoyant affirmation, "And I will dwell in the house of the Lord forever."

Here is a sheep so utterly satisfied with its lot in life, so fully contented with the care it receives, so much "at home" with the shepherd that there is not a shred of desire for a change.

Stated in simple, direct, rather rough ranch language, it would be put like this, "Nothing will ever make me leave this outfit — it's great!"

Conversely, on the shepherd's side there has developed a great affection and devotion to his flock. He would never think of parting with such sheep. Healthy, contented, productive sheep are his delight and profit. So strong, now, are the bonds between them that it is in very truth — forever.

The word "house" used here in the poem has a wider meaning than most people could attach to it. Normally we speak of the house of the Lord as the sanctuary or church or meeting place of God's people. In one sense David may have had this in mind. And, of course, it is pleasant to think that one would always delight to be found in the Lord's house.

But it must be kept in mind always that the Psalmist, writing from the standpoint of a sheep, is reflecting on and recounting the full round of the year's activities for the flock.

He has taken us from the green pastures and still waters of the home ranch, up through the mountain passes onto the high tablelands of the summer range. Fall has come with its storms and rain and sleet that drive the sheep down the foothills and back to the home ranch for the long, quiet winter. In a sense this is coming home. It is a return to the fields and corrals and barns and shelters of the owner's home. During all seasons of the year, with their hazards, dangers, and disturbances, it is the rancher's alertness, care, and energetic management that have brought the sheep through satisfactorily.

It is with a sublime feeling of both composure and contentment that this statement, "I will dwell in the house of the Lord forever," is made.

Actually what is referred to by "house" is the family or household or flock of the Good Shepherd. The sheep is so deeply satisfied with the flock to which it belongs, with the ownership of this particular shepherd, that it has no wish to change whatever.

It is as if it had finally come home again and was now standing at the fence, bragging to its less fortunate neighbors on the other side. It boasts about the wonderful year it has had and its complete confidence in its owner.

Sometimes I feel we Christians should be much more like this. We should be proud to belong to Christ. Why shouldn't we feel free to boast to others of how good our Shepherd is? How glad we should be to look back and recall all the amazing ways in which He has provided for our welfare. We should delight to describe, in detail, the hard experiences through which He has brought us. And we should be eager and quick to tell of our confidence in Christ. We should be bold to state fearlessly that we are so glad we are His. By the contentment and serenity of our lives we should show what a distinct advantage it is to be a member of His "household," of His flock.

I can never meditate on this last phrase in the Psalm without there welling up in my memory vivid scenes from some of the early days on my first sheep ranch.

As winter, with its cold rains and chilling winds came on, my neighbor's sickly sheep would stand huddled at the fence, their tails to the storm, facing the rich fields in which my flock flourished. Those poor, abused, neglected creatures under the ownership of a heartless rancher had known nothing but suffering most of the year. With them there had been gnawing hunger all summer. They were thin and sickly with disease and scab and parasites. Tormented by flies and attacked by predators, some were so weak and thin and wretched that their thin legs could scarcely bear their scanty frames.

Always there seemed to lurk in their eyes the slender, faint hope that perhaps with a bit of luck they could break through the fence or crawl through some hole to free themselves. Occasionally this used to happen, especially around Christmas. This was the time of extreme tides when the sea retreated far out beyond the end of the fence lines which ran down to it. The neighbor's emaciated, dissatisfied, hungry sheep would wait for this to happen. Then at the first chance they would go down on the tidal flats, slip around the end of the fence, and come sneaking in to gorge themselves on our rich green grass.

So pitiful and pathetic was their condition that the sudden feast of lush feed, to which they were unaccustomed, often proved disastrous. Their digestive systems would begin to scour, and sometimes this led to death. I clearly recall coming across three of my neighbor's ewes lying helpless under a fir tree near the fence one drizzly day. They were like three old, limp, gray, sodden sacks collapsed in a heap. Even their bony legs would no longer support them.

I loaded them into a wheelbarrow and wheeled them back to their heartless owner. He simply pulled out a sharp killing knife and slit all three of their throats. He couldn't care less.

What a picture of Satan who holds ownership over so many.

Right there the graphic account Jesus portrayed of Himself as being the door and entrance by which sheep were to enter His fold flashed across my mind.

Those poor sheep had not come into my ranch through the proper gate. I had never let them in.

They had never really become mine. They had not come under my ownership or control. If they had, they would not have suffered so. Even starting out under my management they would have been given very special care.

First they would have been put on dry, limited rations, then they would gradually have been allowed green feed until they were adjusted to the new diet and mode of life.

In short, they tried to get in on their own. It simply spelled disaster. What made it doubly sad was that they were doomed anyway. On the old impoverished ranch they would have starved to death that winter.

Likewise with those apart from Christ. The old world is a pretty wretched ranch, and Satan is a heartless owner. He cares not a whit for men's souls or welfare. Under his tyranny there are hundreds of hungry, discontented hearts who long to enter into the household of God—who ache for His care and concern.

Yet there is only one way into this fold. That way is through the owner, Christ Himself—the Good Shepherd. He boldly declared, "I am the gate; whoever enters through me will be saved. He will come in and go out, and find pasture" (John 10:9).

Almost every day I am literally rubbing shoulders with men and women "on the other side of the fence." What is my impact upon them? Is my life so serene, so satisfying, so radiant because I walk and talk and live with God, that they become envious? Do they see in me the benefits of being under Christ's control? Do they see something of Him reflected in my conduct and character? Does my life and conversation lead them to Him—and thus into life everlasting?

If so, then I may be sure some of them will also long to dwell in the house of the Lord forever. And there is no reason why this cannot happen if they come under His proper ownership.

There is one other beautiful and final sense in which the Psalmist was speaking as a sheep. It is brought out in the Amplified Old Testament where the meaning of this last phrase is, "I will dwell in the 'presence' of the Lord forever."

My personal conviction is that this is the most significant sentiment that David had in his heart as he ended this hymn of praise to divine diligence.

Not only do we get the idea of an ever-present Shepherd on the scene, but also the concept that the sheep wants to be in full view of his owner at all times.

This theme has run all through our studies. It is the alertness, the awareness, the diligence of a never-tiring master which alone assures the sheep of excellent care. And from the sheep's standpoint it is knowing that the shepherd is there; it is the constant awareness of his presence nearby that automatically eliminates most of the difficulties and dangers while at the same time providing a sense of security and serenity.

It is the sheep owner's presence that guarantees there will be no lack of any sort; that there will be abundant green pastures; that there will be still, clean waters; that there will be new paths into fresh fields; that there will be safe summers on the high tablelands; that there will be freedom from fear;

that there will be antidotes for flies and disease and parasites; that there will be quietness and contentment.

In our Christian lives and experience, precisely the same idea and principle applies.

For when all is said and done on the subject of a successful Christian walk, it can be summed up in one sentence. "Live ever aware of God's presence."

There is the "inner" consciousness, which can be very distinct and very real, of Christ's presence in my life, made evident by His gracious Holy Spirit within. It is He who speaks to us in distinct and definite ways about our behavior. For our part it is a case of being sensitive and responsive to that inner voice.

There can be a habitual awareness of Christ within me, empowering me to live a noble and richly rewarding life in cooperation with Him. As I respond to Him and move in harmony with His wishes, I discover that life becomes satisfying and worthwhile. It acquires great serenity and is made an exciting adventure of fulfillment as I progress in it. This is made possible as I allow His gracious Spirit to control, manage, and direct my daily decisions. In fact, I should deliberately ask for His direction even in minute details.

Then there is the wider but equally thrilling awareness of God all around me. I live surrounded by His presence. I am an open person, an open individual, living life open to His scrutiny. He is conscious of every circumstance I encounter. He attends me with care and concern because I belong to Him. And this will continue through eternity. What an assurance!

I shall dwell in the presence of (in the care of) the Lord forever.

Bless His Name.

We want to hear from you. Please send your comments about this book to us in care of zreview@zondervan.com. Thank you.

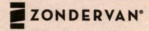

ZONDERVAN.com/
AUTHORTRACKER
follow your favorite authors